GRILLED ☆ Magic

Flavors from the West Coast
By W. Kent Milligan

Canadian Cataloguing in Publication Data

Milligan, W. Kent (William Kent), 1956–

Grilled magic

Includes index
ISBN 0-9681147-0-9

1. Barbecue cookery. 2. Cookery (Smoked foods)
3. Outdoor cookery. I. Title.

TX840.B3M54 1996   641.5'784   C96-910531-2

Launch Books
A Division of Launch Holdings Inc.
#6 - 801 West 1st Street
North Vancouver, British Columbia, Canada V7P 1A4

Tel.: (604) 986-5508   Fax: (604) 984-8709

Printed in Canada by Hignell Printing Limited
Cover and book design by Jennifer Stone, Black Cat Graphics & Communications
Author photograph by R.G. Owen

I would like to thank my wife, Shirley, for her help and patience with this book. Thanks also to Chris and Brad for sampling these recipes!

Contents

How To Use This Book

The recipes in this book have all been tested both on gas and charcoal barbecues. These recipes have been collected from all over the globe or developed by the author. This book has been set up to offer the reader either separate recipes for specific parts of a complete meal or a "feast", as outlined in the feasting section. The detail in this section includes recommendations on wine.

The best part of the barbecue experience is the outdoors, the company and normally, the casual ambience of the event. Please make sure that these things are always present before attempting any recipes in this book! All of these recipes can probably be improved upon, based on your personal preferences and the ambience of the event. Included are many spare pages for your personal comment and alterations to the recipes.

To borrow a phrase, the joy of cooking is the experimentation, that always improving recipe that keeps getting better but is never quite perfect. These recipes are as close as the author has found to perfect. They are very repeatable and always get good reviews.

Enjoy the book, the food, and most importantly, yourselves and company!

Kent Milligan
Author and Barbecueologist
Grilled Magic

5

The Origin Of Barbecuing

Barbecuing, in its truest form, is more an instinct than it is a skill. Around the world, since fire was first discovered and utilized, man has cooked, smoked, or dried meat; or barbecued. The origin of the word is, unfortunately, lost to history. Cowboys used to sleep on Barbecues. Ponce De Leon, the 16th Century Spanish explorer, discovered barbecuing in Haiti and imported this form of cooking to the South-Eastern U.S. when he originally settled that area. A Barbacoa, or lattice-work of thin green sticks, was used over a fire in what is now Louisiana for cooking fish and game. Europeans used to Barb and Que their fowl before cooking it. French settlers to North America dubbed outdoor cooking "de barbe el queue", which literally translates "from whiskers to tail", for the way game was cooked.

Many outdoor feasts I have attended are full of Barbs and Queues!

The tradition we now enjoy in our backyards, at the beach, or wherever, do have meagre beginnings.

Cooking food over a fire is one of the things that we've been doing for hundreds of thousands of years. First, to make tough cuts (I couldn't imagine eating raw Mammoth!) more tender, tastier and easier to chew. Probably more important to our Neolithic cousins was the preservation qualities of cooking, smoking, and drying. If you, until now, thought that a "Barbecue" was throwing a few kneaded ground beef patties on to a Gas-Fired Outdoor Range, then you're not yet in the spirit of things.

Imagine the poor cave man. He has heat and light to see, but suffers the same beast nightly. Winter is just months off and curing is important.

A Barbecue! add a few herbs, grasses, etc. and a feast, rather than the same old venue.

I have often been asked why nobody has a bad time at a Barbecue. My answer is simple. Birds fly south in the winter.

In case you missed that, and I'm absolutely certain you didn't, who can pass up the preparation, viewing, succulent smells, and, the Instinct of a Feast!

6

Getting Started - What You Will Need

The first thing that any burgeoning Barbecuologist will want to consider is his barbecue. Some barbecues will do fine for some things, others are not suitable for some, others are suitable for most. If you don't presently have a barbecue, or, are considering a replacement, please go through this section GETTING STARTED with some detail before you go on a quest.

Most quests are good things to go on, but, not all end the way the storyline was written.

Take these considerations into mind before you buy:

1. Location

Most apartment buildings are not appreciative of a vivacious cook who likes the smell of smoke and the sound of sirens. Hibachis, without the smoke of some barbecues, are good for these locations, or, I shudder to suggest it, but most apartments only allow gas-fired barbecues. So this might be a necessary purchase. Whatever your location for barbecuing, it is only courtesy to ensure the fragrance and smoke of your labors do not pervade the environment of your neighbors – either next-door neighbors or campers. Location in consideration of your environment will ensure "Happy Feasts".

2. Type of Cooking Normally Done

If you are a Burgeoning Barbecuologist and you want to get into some serious feasting then that's a different matter. You can't play tennis with squash balls. You also can't produce a feast, worthy of your skills without the appropriate tools. A smoked salmon on a gas grill comes off like the Gobi desert to a swimmer - a little too dry, perhaps. Conversely, if the outdoor grill is for a family burger or steak feast and little more, no point in buying all the gadgets and, more importantly, the built-in hazards to an efficient, tasty, barbecue.

3. Geography

If Nanook of the North attempted to fire up an Hibachi, all he'd end up with for his trials would be some hot burning coals and a pile of pot metal. Many people who barbecue only use their skills for three to six

months of the year (which, by the way, is a real shame, what better way, in the reaches of winter, to remember the lazy, hazy days.) If this is the case, then different "getting started" codes come into effect.

As I write this, I can make one recommendation. It is better to buy one barbecue for 10 years than one a year for 10 years.

For the easier recipes, any barbecue, even a bucket, will work. If you want to become a master, buy the best and most versatile you can afford. For my money, that's ...

Types of Barbecues

Kettle-Type Barbecues

Yes, for my money, the best. This type of barbecue is easily identifiable by it's shape. The cooking surfaces can be completely closed to enrich the aromas produced by cooking, smoking or drying any variety of foods over a natural heat. This type of barbecue looks like a spaceship with a large under-carriage.

If you find that Barbecuing is not your idea of a good time, these barbecues also double nicely as bird baths or planters. I find these types of barbecues the best all-around barbecues. There are many types of Kettle Barbecues on the market today. Some have variable height grills, heating areas, tilt control, variable speed, overdrive, etc. I think simple is sweet. (With no extra settings and adjustments you tend to learn temperatures and cooking times quickly.) I recommend a solidly built unit of treated metal, or, if you want your unit to last 20 years or more, buy one that is encased, or treated with a good enamel, ceramic or porcelain finish. This finish also serves as a great heat insulator for some of  the harder-to-master barbecuing techniques. Adjustable smoke ports and intake ports in the lid and base of this type of barbecue are necessary to provide a convection-type current of air. This is especially helpful for lighting the coals and adjusting the heat. It is also useful for smoking and long cook-type recipes. The ports are the biggest single feature of a kettle-type barbecue.

If you are considering all types of barbecuing, then, again, I recommend this type of barbecue. Depending on the size bought, anything from two beef patties to a halved Thanksgiving or Christmas turkey can be done. An added feature is that, by fully damping the ports, coals can be reused several times, saving some expense.

Portable Barbecues

The best known of this type is the Hibachi-style of barbecue. The Hibachi now comes in many shapes and sizes. This barbecue is, or was, a traditional outdoors grill for Oriental cooking. It was designed for portability and use outdoors when it was too hot or undesirable to eat indoors. The Japanese made it famous as a "camping implement". Vegetables, chicken, and seafood were all made more edible and hot by its use.

Today, Hibachi-type barbecues outsell anything else by more than 10:1. The down side of these is they are not at all versatile. They grill beef, vegetables and seafood fine. They are not too bad with poultry. They, unfortunately, flare badly. Mostly, they are not very well built. I always have at least one on hand. Normally at least one because the other three are for parts.

Portable barbecues produce a very intense heat over the grill area. Not designed for slow cooking, they are great for searing. As most beach or portable activities call for quickly prepared (always well-prepared) sustenance, these portable units are great for casual barbecuing; best for burgers, wieners, kebabs, etc.

I have found, however, that a well-prepared bed of coals, even from a hardwood fire, with a spare grill produced better, and more enjoyable "portable cookouts" than the use of an Hibachi-style or portable barbecue. If this is to be your purchase, then ensure safe operation by placing the barbecue in or on a safe surface before lighting.

Count your coals so you know how many to use the next time for that particular food. One or two coal variations on these barbecues make a huge heat difference as they are small and designed for grilling, not smoking.

Never use a portable barbecue as a heating device, indoors, or in unventilated areas. If you do survive the toxic fumes that they produce, you will undoubtedly never want to barbecue again.

Any object can be used as a barbecue if you have a grill. A grill, in itself, doesn't have to be a store-bought, super duper, whiz-bang piece of metal. Chicken wire will do. So will old stove grills, chain mail, or expanded metal. In fact, anything metal, with holes in it and no unburnt covering will do. Ensure that the coals, or firebed, can breathe. Gravel, sand, pebbles, dry top soil or the like as a base will offer the proper lungs.

The single biggest drawback of any portable grill is that of uneven cooking. They refuse to produce an even and intense heat on the grill surface, which for many recipes is immediate disaster. With all this said and done, they do in fact serve a use for barbecuing.

Built-In Barbecues

Built-in barbecues offer ... everything, or anything that the true barbecuologist could ever want. Following the natural principal that hot air does, in fact, rise, and, allowing fire to breathe, any design is probably a good one. Assuming good location, a built-in barbecue is the most flexible cookery one could own. If you are planning to install a built-in, remember the four basics: air intake, grill type and height, a lid, and location. There are many excellent plans and books available for the construction of a built-in barbecue, so we won't attempt to be experts of the design or the construction in this book. Just remember one thing ... a built-in is forever. I've seen some beauties but, I have never seen one in use....

Gas/Electric Barbecues

These types of barbecues are marketed with only two things in mind – speed and convenience. As mentioned earlier, if you are the type of backyard cook who wants to throw a couple of steaks, or, some burgers at a barbecue, this is probably the unit for you.

As electric barbecues are more or less a thing of the past, this section will be more directed to gas-fired barbecues, normally propane.

Spits

Truly the oldest of traditional barbecuing, spits are not used as often as in the past. A spit consists of a banked and quieted fire, over which is suspended a pole, or poles containing the food being cooked. Spitted pig, goat, and lamb are still feast material in many parts of the world. This is the easiest type of barbecuing – all you need is a fire, or, large pit, and a lot of time. For a special feast, your guests will never forget this type of outdoor feast.

This truly is the hardest type of outdoor cooking, however. One must tend to the heat of the fire/pit, and continuously watch the food and turn it. With patience and many hours, you will truly be a hit using this technique.

Smokers

Ah! A section to itself!

Smokehood Unit

For "Topless Barbecues", a smokehood can easily be constructed using wire (uncoated coat hangers are good) and heavy-gauge aluminum foil. I strongly recommend against the purchase of a barbecue that is not portable but is priced as such. They rust in a couple of seasons and, even with a smokehood, are completely useless.

Try to buy what feels right but ensure all the necessary features. Try to think of this as a major purchase. The only way to get consistently good results is to be consistent, and that means the right barbecue and the right equipment.

Equipment You Will/Might Need

Because barbecuing is an old art, older than all of the utensils we presently use, very few items are required to produce most of the items in this book. Barbecues, are, by nature, HOT, so watch the fingers, hair, and, after a day in the sun, the forearms, and legs!

Here is a listing of the items you will and might need:

Barbecue Tongs - The most important item. Almost all stores sell them. Make sure they have long handles. I recommend a set that springs open using a doubled-over, or folded, metal where you squeeze to grab and/or release to open. These are cooler to the touch and your fingers won't get jammed up as they might do in the scissor-type.

Spatula - First of all, ALWAYS, at the flipping end, metal. You are pushing it along metal and want a thin surface. Plastic or Teflon won't offer that. Secondly, metal won't melt or impart an unexpected flavor to your feast.

Apron - You don't want: A) grease splatters on your new Hawaiian Shirt do you? B) little burn holes in your outfit? Besides, who will recognize the cook if you're not wearing your uniform. Your guests will quite happily do favors for you if you feign "business" near the grill. The apron helps!

Oven Mitts - These are sometimes useful. Never attempt to pick up a coal with them, though. The above-mentioned tongs and a mitt does help in positioning the grill. After barbecuing, let the grill cool before removing.

A Drink - Because barbecuing is hard work!

Spray Bottle - With water in it, of course. This aids in stopping flare-ups. If you do use this technique, be careful. The steam that will ensue is hot, hot! Use sparingly. (The problem with this technique is the dust flare-up that follows. This unfortunately, can get on your food. Douse the flames by replacing the lid on a kettle-type. On gas barbecues, reposition the food.)

Barbecue Fork or Skewer - Very useful for checking doneness of meats. Also useful for keeping peering, nosey people out of your way! You don't want to share all your recipes do you?

Basting Brush - I prefer to use a long-handled spoon. That way I can pour it on and use the backside of the spoon to spread it around. If you prefer a brush, make sure it isn't plastic, or the like, they melt. Bristle is the best.

There are many other items that do come in useful. If you are using a cutting board to transport your food, make sure you rinse it before you put the cooked food back on it. You and your guests will be much happier, and healthier for it. A resinous-plastic style of board is the best as it doesn't absorb the flavors and smells of your food.

Hinged Grills/Basket - For fish and some other feasts this is an absolute necessity. You can either make your own from two small grills wired together, or spend three weeks trying to find them in a store.

Meat Thermometer - These, generally, are a waste of time on a barbecue. Remember that the ambient temperature changes all over the "body" of the food you are cooking. I would suggest that trial and error and recording the results is a much more successful method of "doneness".

Grill Cleaner - Never use a chemical unless you wash very thoroughly. The heat of your barbecue will sterilize the grill. A little scrape with a spatula is all that is generally required.

Producing Heat, and . . .

There are some general hints and safety precautions listed here to ensure that your barbecues will all be without any incident, except a food riot to get more of the succulent feast you have just prepared.

If you are barbecuing in a campground, at the beach, or, for that matter, not in your own familiar backyard, make sure of the terrain you plan to set your portable chuck wagon up in. Sparks and not-entirely-out bits of coal create a horrifying spectacle if they light on dry grass, leaves, or dry vegetation. Make sure, as well, that the wind is to your back. You don't want those sparks lighting you. The smell of the smoke might not be too amenable a few hours after the feast, either!

Never use any kind of charcoal or gas grills indoors, or in confined spaces. Both produce noxious gases than can do very serious damage.

Be wary of flare-ups caused by fat and juices dripping onto the coals or lava rocks. If you have a hooded barbecue, starve the coals. This will put out the fire flare-up. If you don't have a hood, raise the grill and carefully reposition the meat. Minor flare-ups can be handled with a fine spray from a spray bottle of water. Ensure this bottle never contained anything but water, or wash it very well as some odors of prior contents may taint your feast.

If you have a kettle or gas barbecue, damp the unit. With gas, shut down about 10 minutes after you finish. This, with the gas and kettle will help clean the grill. Never dump hot coals out of a barbecue – something will get burnt.

If you must douse your barbecue after cooking, use these methods. They are not only safest, but easiest on your barbecue. First, remove the grill(s) and set them safely aside to cool. Bunch the coals into a loose pile. Gently trickle water over them, watching the steam carefully so you don't get burnt. Rustle the coals and repeat. Dump the coals into an area that won't cause a mess, not a garbage bag, and fully douse coals to ensure none are still alive – remember one live coal could restart the whole bunch.

Some people rescue wetted coals after drying. The astringent that holds briquettes together, however, is water soluble. I find that once-wetted coals fall apart too readily – not producing a reliable heat. With this in mind, I would recommend against using them.

14

Lighting Gas Ranges

This is a simple matter with gas barbecues. **Always read the manufacturer's suggested starting practices, this is a guide only!** Always turn the supply nozzle full on before you attempt to light. The firing jets are designed to offer the best performance at this setting. You will not save any gas or money by not following this, and it could be hazardous. Light the gas either using the spark generator or a match. Keep your face and body away from the barbecue, as it will "whoosh" to life and might singe hair, eyebrows or arms. Let the barbecue, with the lid down, warm up for at least 5 minutes (10 plus is better) before you start to cook. After you are finished cooking, turn the setting(s) back to full, put the lid back down and let your unit self-clean for a minimum of 5 minutes (depending on what you've cooked, anything with marinades leave longer) before turning off.

Lighting Charcoal Barbecues

There are many techniques to getting a good bed of coals going, and within a good time period. Always start your coals at least twenty minutes before you want to start cooking. Almost every barbecuologist I know (including myself) expects a beautiful bed 5 minutes after lighting, which is usually 10 minutes before everybody wants to eat. Prepare your bed in advance using one of the following methods.

If you are barbecuing on a fire pit, or an open area, a fire chimney is probably your best bet. Use a large (32 oz or bigger) tin with holes punched in the top and the bottom removed. Fill with coals and up-end, sealed (punched) end up over lighting materials or more coals with lighting materials. The warm air rising draft will set up a current that will light the coals quickly. Be careful when you remove the tin, it'll be hot! Next build a pyramid with the hot coals on the bottom. Spread them out when they are at least 60% grey or glowing.

Always make sure, no matter what your barbecue arrangement is, that the coals can "breathe" from beneath.

If you use solid lighter fuel for your barbecue, your choice is excellent. Place chunks about mid-tier – inward in a pyramid of coals. Light and leave. When the adjacent coals are turning at least 20% grey or glowing, build a series of smaller pyramids over these. This will have

15

uniformity of coal size, therefore heat, and speed up the setting of the coals.

Liquid starters, never gas, ether, coal oil, naphtha, or the like; are still available. I, personally, don't recommend them, as they are dangerous in the wrong hands and do, as a by-product, produce some noxious gases. They do, however, light coals. Spray on generously to a pyramid-like stack of coals. Make sure the coals are not live. Let the liquid soak in for about 30 seconds, and light. If a second soaking is required for the coals to take hold, repeat, ensuring any lit coals are removed from the second soaking. As with solid starters, make smaller pyramids over the lit coals, once they are established.

By far the easiest briquette lighting technique, at least in your backyard, is the electric starter. These are readily available, fast and safe. Place the starter either on the insulating material of the barbecue, or rest it on a small bed of coals. Build a pyramid on top, and plug in. Leave the starter for 5 to 10 minutes, or until there is a small visual flame around the inner coals. Unplug and remove the starter to a place of un-burnable safety (or to the far edge of the barbecue) for about 10 minutes. Rebuild the pyramid with as broad a base of well-established coals as possible.

When all the coals are grey, and you are ready to cook, spread the coals with even spacing over the bottom of the barbecue. The grey ash on the coals will insulate the heat into the coals so give them a gentle rustle now and then, if you desire more heat. Place the grill over the coals and let it cure for a few minutes before you clean or oil the grill.

This probably sounds like a week's preparation for one outdoor meal, but it really isn't. As you will notice after a couple of events, you've probably only spent an actual 10 minutes to get to this point. (I, on the other hand, have spent countless hours.)

Maintenance

Very little maintenance is required of a reasonable quality barbecue. Keep it out of the elements if you're not going to use it for extended periods of time. Or, keep it covered. Don't keep the grill sparkling clean! This will lead to rust and mildew contamination. A covering of

grease and oils protects all the internal surfaces of a barbecue. A good cleaning should be done only about once a year and never at the end of a season. If you aren't going to use your barbecue for an extended period, meaning a few months, make sure to store the grill(s) in a dry, cool area. Never sandpaper or use a grit to make your grill sparkle. Your food will taste yuck, and stick for a long period thereafter. Also, the grill's life expectancy will drop.

Make sure a coal-type barbecue is clean of ash on a regular basis. The ash is slightly caustic – especially wet – and will cut down on life expectancy. It also acts as an insulator and does not reflect heat. Keep the outside free of rust spots, or touch them up. As with a car, rust will eat your entire barbecue within a couple of seasons if unchecked! This, again, is a good reminder why a well-finished barbecue is probably the best of buys.

If you have a gas barbecue, the only additional maintenance are the gas lines and the lava rocks. Make sure that all lines are in good order. If there are any crimps in the lines, or you hear hissing at a coupling, tighten or replace immediately. All gases are dangerous if not treated properly. Never attempt to refill a tank that is disposable. Once a year make up a soapy solution and check for bubbles at all points. Clean out any accumulated grease at the bottom periodically. This grease could light, causing burning drips to ooze out the bottom and get to the hoses. The lava rocks supplied do wear out. This is due to the repeated heat/cool cycle and all of the grease and juice drippings that attack it. Lava rocks, or the synthetic versions, are initially very porous. This is why they react so like briquettes. These should be replaced periodically, depending on usage. Never wash the rocks with any cleaning agents as this will contaminate your food. As a matter of fact, when the rocks are dirty, they just should be replaced for optimum barbecue usage.

General maintenance, as in kitchen cutlery, should be observed with all barbecue utensils. If you are using a grill basket (see GRILLS) do not wash with soap. Otherwise, that, in a nutshell, is maintenance. Much less labor-intensive than most of our modern-day appliances.

What to Put on the Barbecue

Grill and Kebab Selection

This is a subject that few even give thought to. It is, perhaps, one of the most important aspects of true barbecuology. I have a good selection of these and quite often forget where I've left them to cool – to the chagrin of wife, family, and neighbors. For basic recipes, the Grill you use will be the one that arrived with the barbecue. You can add heating racks, which fit onto your existing surface allowing the food to cook while heating takes place. Fish baskets, wiener baskets, chestnut baskets ... The choice, if you go to a good barbecue supply house (like the one that sold you this book) are endless. A word of warning ... don't go overboard as a multi-purpose rack may serve many functions. Your imagination will serve you well here. Outlined below are the more important types of grills, spits, and kebabs that you should be aware of for specialty barbecuing. Remember, you have more than one pot in your kitchen so you should consider more than one grill.

Fish Grill - These are two grills that are hinged at one end and have two long handles with a fastening device at the other. When barbecuing fish or other types of food requiring either flipping (with a delicate meat) or holding in place (because of size) this type of grill is a necessity. Don't buy the type that have outlines of fish, or other items in them unless necessary, as the flexibility decreases with this design.

Basting Grill - Some foods require a long time in the barbecue without being close to the heat source for the entire time. A two-tiered barbecue rack allows the rotation of this food with a sustained, non-direct heat rack on the top and a direct heat rack on the bottom. This is called a Basting Grill as the top rack food bastes the bottom (basting is performed on food on top and gravity does the rest). These grills only work well in covered barbecues as convection ensures heat to the top rack.

Heating Grill - Heating grills are quite often supplied with original equipment. These are quite like basting grills except usually attached at the periphery of the main grill and not over it. These are great for defrosting buns, bread, etc. The other advantage of these is multi-item barbecues. You can place almost-done items, like roasted corn, onions, etc. on these and serve all at the same time.

Aluminum Foil - This is not normally thought of as a grill, but truly it is. Many items like potatoes, vegetables, even quick-rising breads or bannocks can be co-cooked with your meat if you use this handy invention. Remember that if you seal the foil, steam will evacuate when you open it. Be careful to avoid burns. Remember, too, that you get what you pay for – the best quality is definitely worthwhile.

There are many other grills and baskets available. The above I find to be the most important and the rest you may find very useful.

Spits/Kebabs - These two, although quite different cooking techniques, are spun together as the end result is the same. To produce a succulent food morsel that is not over- or under-cooked, but more importantly, is not burnt. This cooking technique is quite definitely the most time honored of all outdoor cooking methods. Remember the raw mammoth? Anyway, refinement is part of human nature and that is also true of both of these cooking or barbecuing methods. A spit can be made of a green stick. Never cut a tree down to make one. Scrub brush produces the best green sticks as they are a very hard wood and generally do not burn very readily. Never use evergreen boughs for this as they are resinous, burn quickly and impart an unwanted flavor to food. (Similarly, never spit-cook or barbecue over evergreen boughs.) Spits are also commercially available for larger cookouts, either as a motorized rotisserie, or hand-cranked, for larger meats. Spits can handle feasts as large as a side of beef. Spitting requires a lot of patience and time. Meat cooks from the outside in, and the fat content insulates cooking as the heat penetrates. This means that spit cooking requires lower heat and longer time for cooking. Spits are easy to make, one warning though, slow cooking requires absolute cleanliness of the spit. Also, more patience is needed than most of us ever had ... even before children.

Kebabs, like the phraseology barbecue, have beginnings lost to us all. A kebab is an eastern way of preparing meats and vegetables over an open cooking fire, very much related to spitting, but generally on a smaller scale. Kebabs, traditionally, are long barbs, less than a foot, that hold beef, pork, lamb or chicken. These generally also hold portions of vegetables and the like. Kebab barbs are generally available in high chrome metals. Traditionally they were wood and these are also readily available. Never re-use wood kebabs and ensure that metal versions are kept extremely clean.

A general note on grills is that with the exception of kebabs and spits, the surfaces are exposed to the outer side of food. The barbecue is a natural sterilizer, as the heat from the heat source exterminates all of the nasties that can contaminate the grill surfaces. Always ensure adequate temperature and time to allow this to happen. A rule of thumb is that if there's sufficient heat to cook the food, your barbecue grill is sterilized. Stay away from using any cleaning agents on your grills, with the obvious exception of spits and grills. All too often a bitter barbecue is the result of cleaning agents contaminating the food. Food contamination is handled below.

Care of Food

A very important aspect of outdoor cooking is ensuring it is not, or does not, become contaminated between the fridge and the barbecue. There are many contaminants that can affect the flavor of your food, but these generally are not harmful to whoever eats them. The major concern in the handling or cooking of any foods, either barbecue, or in the kitchen, is food poisoning. There are a group of viruses, fungi, and bacteria that cause these. By far the worst with reference to barbecuing is Salmonella. Salmonella is generally present on many foods and is not a problem unless the food is mishandled. This bacteria breeds rapidly between 50° and 110° F. Care then should be taken to ensure that the food to be cooked goes directly from the fridge or cooler to the barbecue. Temperatures exceeding 150° F will destroy this bacteria and ensure the food is sterile for eating. Cooked meat can be recontaminated by coming in contact with uncooked meat, dirty utensils, uncooked meat juices, etc. A safety list will assure you of no problems with respect to this and other contaminants. If you follow these general rules then safety is pretty much guaranteed.

1. Keep all the foods you are going to eat (perishables) below 40° F. This is inclusive of salads, dressings, desserts, etc. If picnicking or camping, ensure the cooler is well insulated and out of the sun.

2. When transferring from fridge/cooler to barbecue or table, try not to leave the food out very long before serving.

3. Ensure that all cooking utensils, serving platters, etc. are thoroughly cleaned between handling of uncooked and cooked foods.

4. Don't let cooked meats come into contact with uncooked meats.

5. The foods to watch most closely include: poultry, pork, fish, chopped/ground meats, offal, eggs, and prepared salads and dressings.

The following symptoms could point toward food poisoning. If these symptoms appear in more than one person eating together, chances are poisoning has occurred. This can be anywhere from very mild poisoning to very serious. Symptoms will start to appear anytime after three hours of infection and up to 72 hours after. Take special care with older, younger, or already ill persons. A physician or the hospital should be at least contacted if symptoms persist or deteriorate. For mild cases (and we will all suffer this at some point in our lives – probably from a roadside restaurant) take lots of clear or semi-clear fluids to replace those that you most definitely will lose in other manners and complain bitterly – you're allowed at least that!

Symptoms include:

1. Cramps or cramping
2. Diarrhoea and vomiting
3. Intestinal gas
4. Nausea and headaches*
5. Fever and delirium*
6. Excessive Salivation*

*If any of these occur, seek medical attention immediately.

Additional Food care techniques will ensure successful cookouts every time.

Make sure no burnt-on bits are left on the grill before barbecuing – this makes the food taste better.

Make sure that all fish are completely cleaned and properly preserved before using.

The other rules are general and the same you would follow in your kitchen. The name of the game is freshness!

Smoking

A lot of time is not going to be spent on this chapter with reference to the art of smoking for preservation of foodstuffs, or as the primary preparation method for food. The chief difference between barbecuing food and smoking it is time. The art of smoking dates back long before any records exist. The two chief reasons for smoking of foodstuffs were for preservation and flavor. The smoking process creates a glazing of the meat, poultry or fish being treated which protects it from the bacteria that sour and/or taint it. This, therefore, increases the "shelf-life" of it. If, however, the smoking process is incorrectly performed, or, not long enough, all of the regular problems will arise. In fact, improperly smoked food may enhance the dangers of contamination rather than getting rid of them.

With reference to this book, smoke is used as a flavor enhancer and/or a finishing agent. Many good books on cold and hot smoking are available if you are interested in pursuing this aspect of "cooking".

One of the natural by-products of barbecuing is smoke. This is the key ingredient in making a barbecue a complete taste success. Too much smoke can add a salty or overpowering flavor to a barbecue dish. The thing to remember when using smoke to finish a dish is that smoky flavor "builds" with time. That is to say, some smoke produces a certain smoky flavor, a little more time produces a lot more smoke flavor, so, when first experimenting with this, too little is definitely better than too much!

There are many packaged wood chips/coals which can be used for smoking. Mesquite is probably the most popular "craze" smoke flavor of recent times. Prior to that hickory was the favorite. There are many types now available and all add a certain charm. There is a partial list of what is available below, with a suggestion of the results you can anticipate and the food that works best with that particular smoke. Generally, hardwoods work best. NEVER use pine or cedar (evergreens) as the pitch in the wood can cause a fire hazard and the chips burn sooty, causing a sooty, bitter coating on the food you are smoking. Eucalyptus is not a good choice either.

Wetting the chips before using adds some moisture with the smoke being produced – this can help keep some foods moist. It also extends the life of the chips.

The Smoking Procedures that follow the chart are general in nature. Experimentation is the best bet here as conditions are just too variable to make any firm recommendations.

Chip Species	Flavor(s) Imparted	Type of Food
MESQUITE (chips or coals)	Adds a "sweet bite" to foods. Enhances some herbs/spices such as garlic, rosemary, and oregano.	Works extremely well with barbecued steaks, burgers (beef in general), also good with chicken.
HICKORY (chips or shavings) (essence is available – use sparingly)	Adds a bittersweet flavor to meats and vegetables. Use sparingly over long cooking period.	Good with poultry, pork, and some vegetables, especially potatoes. Excellent used in conjunction with alder for fish.
ALDER (chips or shavings)	Adds a light smoky flavor, a touch of sweetness and salt. Can be used more liberally than other chips.	Excellent with fish (can add a touch of Hickory to enhance). Also excellent with poultry and pork; with a marinade.
FRUIT (Apple, Cherry, etc) (chips or shavings; never branch parts)	Adds a sweet-ish flavor, with a slight essence of fruit tree being used, especially apple which is most popular	Excellent with fish (firm-bodied) also excellent with pork.
MAPLE (chips or shavings)	Can be overpowering if used too much, also can be quite bitter. Imparts a bitter-musty flavor.	Excellent for grilling nuts and sweet meats especially good with ham and fatty cuts of meat.
BIRCH (chips or shavings never bark)	Used very sparingly, adds a nice touch of smoke.	Used sparingly imparts a nice background to all spicy foods.

23

Smoking Procedures

If you are going to brine your food before smoking, use the brine only the once and ensure all normal cleanliness steps are performed.

Continue all cooking and smoking procedures to completion, don't start/stop this process.

Make sure you keep the heat in the fire/barbecue. Remember that smoke in itself is heat and if you don't replenish the chips/shavings the appropriate curing will not take place.

As temperatures and smoke denseness cannot be measured, all smoking/curing times are based on trial and error. This is also true with moisture contents.

The relative humidity of the ambient climate has more to do with the finished product than anything else. Remember to decrease humidity as the process takes place. Do not add additional moisture in any form to the finishing product.

Smoking, in our Western area, includes the smoking of both fish species and beef/beef derivatives such as Buffalo, etc. The two best known of all of these are Smoked Salmon (fish) and Pemmican (Jerky). These two foodstuffs were staples throughout the year and the original recipes for these quite unsavory to the epicure. The salmon (fish) tended to sweat oil and salt and the pemmican tended to toughness (somewhat like sinew or dog suets). The taste of these, however, was exquisite. The spicing was wild in nature (dill for salmon; berries, sage, thyme, and broom for pemmican).

So, when cooking and smoking in more modern times, utilize the freezer for life, cut back on the salt and drying and use all of the spices, herbs and even some of the marinades that you use for everyday cooking. Just cut back on the overall cooking time, temperature and coax some smoky flavor into your dish.

Barbecues can reach temperatures regularly exceeding 400° F (205° C). Remember when smoking or smoke-finishing you want to use a lower temperature with the smoke, for a longer period of time. This means that if you are smoke-finishing, you should lower the temperature for approximately the last half or two-thirds of the cooking time (except all poultry) and add the smoke. Smoke is a little like a marinade in that it coats what you are cooking. If you cut back on the temperature, you have some "room" for cooking longer, without over-cooking. Make sure you watch to ensure the food doesn't dry out. Smoking can and will enhance all foods that you cook outdoors. Experimentation will make your foods tasty and always a delightful adventure.

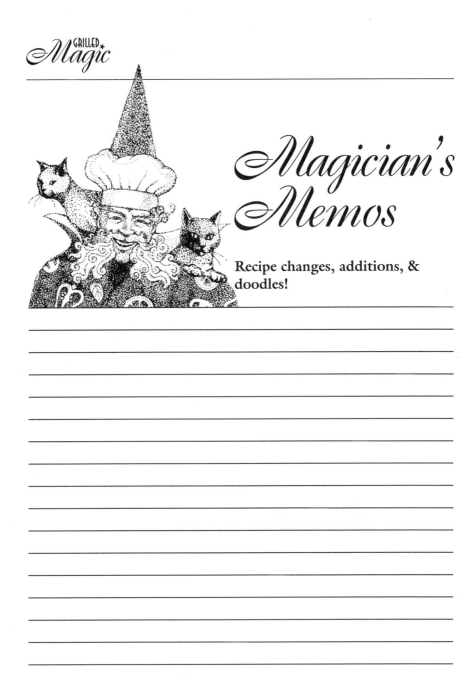

GRILLED
Magic

Magician's Memos

Recipe changes, additions, & doodles!

Feasting

Barbecued Salmon Feast

Barbecued Salmon Feast

Serves 6 - 8 people

The Wine

Start with a lighter bodied Chardonnay. This will go best with the appetizer and will pique the palate for the main course. For the Main Course, a full bodied Chardonnay, or, if you want to be different, a light Pinot Noir is a good bet.

The Appetizer(s)

Choose either the Clam Soup by itself, or, the others as you wish. The Clam Soup is quite complex and filling so is nicely followed with one of the two Salads listed. Additionally, the Clam Soup is better when the temperatures are a little cooler.

The Vegetables

The Vegetables are all selected for color – to visually improve the meal layout. Rice, either Brown Rice of the Wild Rice Casserole listed are my recommendations for the final "touch".

The Plan

Prepare and serve appetizer(s) and wine. Make sure fish and rice dishes are prepared. The rice will take the longest so, if you want a relaxed and progressive meal, ensure enough time for all. Approximate preparation times and cooking times are included.

Appetizers

Clam Soup

1 - 2 lbs clams - aspirated (see "CLAM PREPARATION")
1 cooking onion, very coarsely chopped
½ cup butter or 2 Tbsp olive oil and ⅓ cup margarine
¼ cup each green & red peppers, cut in fine lengths
¼ - ½ cup white wine
¼ cup cold water
Pinch garlic powder
Pinch chili powder
½ cup chopped green onions
¼ tsp oregano
⅛ tsp ground coriander
Parsley to garnish
Salt to taste (very little needed)

In a large container, melt butter at medium temperature. Add and sauté chopped onions. Add all spices except coriander and parsley, then add and lightly sauté green and red peppers. Quench all heat by adding wine and cold water. Bring to light boil and add clams. Bring back to boil - don't increase to full heat - and cover. Cook 5 - 8 minutes. If and when shells are open, it is ready to serve, if shells don't open, don't serve. Serve in tureens with bread or buns and butter. Many of your guests will also enjoy the broth served with the clams.

Cooking time, less preparation time for this is approximately 20 minutes.

Clam Preparation

When buying the clams, pick for freshness. Your nose will help you with this selection. Clams filter sand so will naturally still have a few particles in them when you get them home. For best results, place them in a large tub of cold water with some ice. An hour or two of this will allow the clams to dispose of the bit of sand they still have in them. Before cooking the clams, be sure to remove any seaweed or other materials stuck to the shell. Finally, a light scrubbing of the shell is useful for the very best results.

Scallops & Bacon

¼ - ½ lb medium or smaller scallops
½ lb bacon strips, cut in half
¼ cup tomato ketchup
¼ cup medium-hot horseradish
dash lemon juice
dash Worcestershire sauce

These can be done on the grill or in the oven on broil. The oven takes ⅓ again as long. If you use the grill, a basket or long kebabs should replace the toothpicks.

¼ - ½ lbs medium or smaller scallops. Wrap scallops with bacon and hold in place with toothpicks or skewers. Turn often until bacon is cooked then serve - if they are on a skewer, you should remove and place on a plate for serving.

The dipping sauce for the above is produced by adding approximately equal portions of tomato ketchup and medium-hot horseradish. Complement this with a couple of drops of fresh lemon juice and Worcestershire sauce.

Sauce preparation time: 2 - 5 minutes

Scallop cooking time: 8 - 15 minutes

Garlic Prawns

1 - 2 lbs peeled prawns (cooked)
⅛ - ¼ cup butter or 2 Tbsp olive oil and ¼ cup margarine
1 clove garlic, finely chopped
Lemon or lime juice

Heat butter or oil/margarine combination to medium high (it shouldn't smoke). Add 1 clove finely chopped garlic and then 2 drops lemon or lime juice. Add prawns and sauté 30 - 40 seconds and turn over for same time then turn off heat. When mixture is sufficiently cool, or within 60 - 90 seconds, remove and serve.

Total cooking time: approximately 3 minutes

Fresh Grilled Prawns

Approximately ½ - 1 lb fresh un-peeled large to medium prawns

Place prawns on skewers and grill each side approximately 1 minute, turning twice. "Paint" prawns each turn with one of two sauces listed below.

Lemon Garlic Sauce

⅛ - ¼ cup melted butter
1 - 2 cloves garlic
dash chili or specialty pepper

Mix melted butter with 1 - 2 cloves well-crushed garlic. Sprinkle with a dash of chili or specialty pepper.

Plum Lime Garlic Sauce

¼ cup plum sauce or plum chutney
Juice of ½ lime
2 Tbsp olive oil
1 clove garlic, crushed

Combine plum sauce or chutney, lime juice, olive oil and crushed garlic in a bowl.

As above, paint every turn.

An additional small amount of these sauces can be added after cooking. Don't overdo though.

Cracked Crab

This is served cold. Buy fresh cooked crab legs. Ensure the legs are cracked before you serve so no one will cut themselves on the shell.

Kent's Seafood Sauce

1 cup Ketchup
2 Tbsp Worcestershire sauce
4 Tbsp hot horseradish
Squirt of fresh lemon juice

The Salad

A Sauvignon Blanc/Fumé Blanc or the lighter Chardonnay is the wine pick for this course.

Crab Spinach Salad

Spinach
¼ lb cooked crab
¼ lb imitation crab
Italian or oil & vinegar dressing

Fresh shredded spinach that is cold is covered with approximately ¼ pound or less of clean cooked crab and ¼ pound of imitation crab. Put the dressing on just before service and keep it quite light. Dressing: Use an Italian-style dressing or vinegar and oil (equal proportions) with a few drops (2 - 3) of lemon. Add some fresh ground pepper.

Traditional Caesar Salad

Use the Caesar dressing sparingly.

¼ cup oil
1 clove garlic, crushed
3 - 5 anchovies
2 - 3 Tbsp lemon juice
1 egg, raw or cooked gently for 60 - 90 seconds
¼ cup Parmesan cheese
1 head romaine lettuce, washed and dried
croutons
Parmesan cheese

Put the oil, garlic, anchovies, lemon juice, egg, and ¼ cup Parmesan cheese in a blender and blend at high speed until combined and fairly thick. Break up the romaine lettuce and place in a large salad bowl. Just before serving, add croutons and Parmesan cheese to taste, and just enough dressing to lightly coat the lettuce.

The Vegetables

As mentioned earlier, the vegetables that go with the salmon are chosen for their presentation qualities. Sliced carrots and celery are inter-mingled, 2 - 3 of each, on the plate. Add cherry tomatoes or tomato wedges and finish with a piece of raw or slightly blanched cauliflower.

The Rice

Rice works extremely well with barbecued salmon. My favorite is a wild rice/brown rice combination. An acceptable short-cut that shortens preparation time are the combination rice packages readily available at the supermarket. Stay away from anything too spicy or ethnic as they will ruin the delicate flavors of the fish.

Kent's Wild & Brown Rice Combo

½ cup wild rice
1 cup brown rice
¼ tsp savory
¼ tsp thyme
½ tsp oregano
½ cup white wine
¼ cup butter

Put wild rice in a large container of water and let stand ½ hour. Rinse rice well. Replace water and bring rice to a boil. Leave rice on a low boil for 10 minutes. Turn off and let stand for 10 - 20 minutes. Rinse well and add brown rice. Add savory and thyme as well as oregano. Add white wine and butter. Follow standard cooking procedures for 1 cup brown rice. After cooking, add salt to taste.

Approximate Preparation time, start to finish: ½ hours

Approximate Total Cooking time: 1 hour 25 minutes.

The Salmon

Enclosed are two recipes. The "White" is a traditional style that all will love. The "Red" is non-traditional, and people will either love it or ....

For a change of pace, I often will cook and serve both at the same time. This is easy to do if you choose fillets or butterfly the fish instead of using a whole salmon. Remember, though, a fillet will dry out quicker than a whole salmon. Cooking times and temperatures are critical for cuts versus whole fish.

Barbecued Salmon

Allow approximately ½ pound per person of whole salmon, slightly more for cuts of salmon. Whole salmon can be de-boned, but I prefer bone in. The skeletal structure transmits heat and helps the salmon cook faster, thus decreasing the chance of over-cooking and drying out.

To open the fish, butterfly-like, take a sharp knife and cut the fish along one side of the backbone on the inside. Once cooked, the bones are easily removed using a fork. Slide the fork under the row of bones and twist. The bones will easily pop out of the flesh and then can be removed. Be very careful with the bones with very young or old people. The whole section can be removed in one piece on the side of the fish that has a backbone intact. Leave the skin intact.

Place the fish, skin down on one side of the fish basket. Pour on sauce liberally, close basket and cook. The fish should be cooked mostly on the skin side, you only flip onto sauce side for 2 - 3 minutes when the fish is almost done. There is no way to gauge the actual cooking time as it is so variable with weight, temperature and species of salmon. The flesh will flake easily and be quite firm to the touch when cooked. A little experience will teach a lot here. A medium hot fire is the best for Barbecued Salmon. Serve whole without the skin on.

"White" Sauce

1 egg yolk
½ cup mayonnaise
Juice of 1 lemon
1 - 2 Tbsp dill
¼ cup cooking oil
½ onion, chopped, approximately ½ cup

In a mixing bowl add: Yolk of one egg, mayonnaise, lemon juice, and dill. Blend together gently adding cooking oil as you are blending. Blend until thick and fold in the chopped onion. Spread generously over flesh side of salmon. Barbecue as above, white sauce will adhere, turn and cook to a light brown when ready.

Preparation time: 10 - 15 minutes.

"Red" Sauce

3 - 5 garlic cloves, well crushed
3 - 4 sun-dried tomatoes, finely chopped
½ cup olive oil

Combine in a bowl the crushed garlic cloves, sun-dried tomatoes, and olive oil. Mix together. Paint onto flesh side of salmon. Cook as above. Garlic will be cooked when ready.

Preparation time: 10 - 15 minutes.

The Dessert

After all of this, dessert should be light. A fruit salad or fresh berries will make an excellent finish.

Magician's Memos

Recipe changes, additions, & doodles!

Chicken & Rib Feast

Chicken & Rib Feast

Serves 8 - 10 people

These two backyard favorites, when combined with all the trappings, will create memories not often forgotten.

The Wine

A crisp Sauvignon Blanc or Fumé Blanc are great with this feast. Zinfandel is also excellent, but can overshadow the chicken.

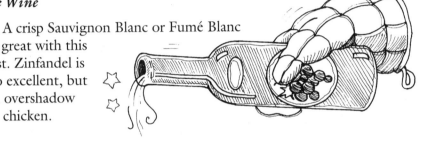

The Appetizer(s)

Tortilla chips with a spicy salsa really set the mood for this type of meal. A vegetable tray used as an appetizer and then refreshed to go with the meal is also excellent.

The Salads & Vegetable(s)

A potato salad and coleslaw look great and complement the main course. This and the vegetable tray are probably enough to complete this meal.

The Plan

Prepare the salads in advance as they take the longest to prepare. Make sure they stay properly cool until they are ready to be served.

The Salads & Vegetables

Potato Salad

2 ½ cup diced cold cooked potatoes
1 tsp sugar
1 tsp vinegar
½ cup onion, chopped
1 ½ tsp salt
1 ½ tsp chopped parsley
¾ cup mayonnaise
2 hard-boiled eggs, sliced

Combine sugar and vinegar and sprinkle over potatoes. Add the rest of the ingredients, being careful with the egg slices. Serve in lettuce lined bowl. Garnish with radishes, parsley, watercress, cucumber slices and egg slices.

For something different you could add ½ cup sliced celery, and/or ¼ cup coarsely chopped sweet pickles.

Make sure to keep this cold until serving time.

Preparation time: Approximately 15 minutes.

Coleslaw

½ - 1 whole green cabbage
½ onion, diced, approximately
Mayonnaise or "Miracle Whip"
Paprika

Cut the green cabbage cut into strips approximately 1" long and approximately ⅛" wide. Place cut up cabbage in a bowl and add diced onion. Add enough mayonnaise or "Miracle Whip" to lightly coat all the cabbage. Sprinkle with paprika, mix all together well and refrigerate until time to eat.

Preparation time: Approximately 15 minutes.

Dips for Vegetable Tray

Onion Dip

Makes 2 cups

1 envelope Lipton Onion Soup Mix
1 cup plain yogurt
1 cup light sour cream

Combine all ingredients and let sit in the refrigerator for approximately 2 hours for flavors to meld.

Herb Dip

Makes 2 cups
1 cup plain yogurt
1 cup light sour cream
2 Tbsp chopped parsley
2 Tbsp chopped chives
1 tsp fines herbs
$\frac{1}{8}$ tsp curry powder
$\frac{1}{4}$ tsp paprika
dash salt

Combine all ingredients and let sit in the refrigerator for approximately 2 hours for flavors to meld.

Horseradish Dipping Sauce

Makes 1 cup

1 cup light sour cream
2 tsp horseradish, or to taste
1 green onion, minced

Combine all ingredients and let sit in the refrigerator for approximately 2 hours for flavors to meld.

The Ribs

The ribs will take more preparation than the chicken so, the morning of your barbecue you should start getting this part organized.

3 - 4 lbs pork baby back ribs
¼ tsp sage
¼ tsp savory
½ tsp oregano
½ tsp garlic powder or 3 garlic cloves, well crushed

This recipe calls for 3 - 4 pounds of pork baby back ribs. Cut each into approximate 3" lengths. In a large pot add enough water to cover and boil ribs. Then add sage, savory, oregano and either the garlic powder or the crushed cloves of garlic. Boil until the pork is tender (it will start to "roll" away from the bones). Place the ribs in a bowl with a light covering of marinade and refrigerate until you are ready to grill.

Marinade

This marinade contains sugar and honey. Both of these burn off and char easily on the barbecue. When you "paint" the ribs with this, turn very often and keep to the cooler edges of the barbecue. If you are cooking only the ribs, a medium to light fire is a good choice.

Mix together:

¼ cup soy sauce
5 Tbsp honey
2 Tbsp brown sugar
½ tsp salt
1 Tbsp oil
2 crushed garlic cloves
1 cup chicken stock or prepared stock
small pinch cayenne pepper

Put the ribs on the barbecue without any marinade. Turn them a couple of times before starting to use the marinade. Paint the marinade on, you are building a glaze, so you will require numerous coatings. As mentioned earlier, turn often so the ribs don't burn. When ready, let stand for a few minutes before serving or, store and re-warm when the chicken is ready.

The Chicken

2 lbs chicken parts
¾ tsp Worcestershire sauce
½ cup soy sauce
pinch garlic powder
½ cup saki
2 finely chopped green onions
4 Tbsp honey or brown sugar*
5 Tbsp ketchup or 2 Tbsp ketchup and 3 Tbsp plum sauce

*If you use brown sugar, melt in ¼ cup of hot water

Add all ingredients together except honey and ketchup. Pour over chicken parts in a glass or non-metal tray. Place on stove top and bring to a boil. Place all in the oven at 350°F. Turn after ½ hour. Once flipped, turn off oven and remove chicken.

Drain off liquid into a saucepan after the ½ hour and reduce to ½ the volume. Add the honey and ketchup to the saucepan at this point. While the liquid is reducing, put the chicken on the barbecue. Turn often watching carefully for flare-ups. The chicken will drop a lot of juices at the start, which will burn, so watch this carefully. When the meat starts to firm, after approximately 10 minutes, start to paint the chicken with the reduced sauce. Turn often so the sauce won't burn. Another 20 minutes or so and the chicken will be finished. To check, stick a fork into the meat and twist. The meat should slightly "flake" and come away cleanly from the bones.

Magician's Memos

Recipe changes, additions, & doodles!

Big Ranch Barbecue Feast

Big Ranch Barbecue Feast

Serves up to 20 people

The Wine

Start with a lighter-bodied Pinot Noir or a French Burgundy. For white wine drinkers, a full-bodied Chardonnay is a good bet.

The Appetizer(s)

As this particular feast is very casual, the appetizers chosen below are suggested to set the mood for the feast.

The Appetizers

Tortilla Chips & Salsa

Hot Salsa

Makes about 6 ½ cups

10 fresh plum tomatoes, peeled and coarsely chopped
2 cups canned tomatoes, coarsely chopped
8 cloves garlic, minced
2 medium onions, 1 minced and 1 coarsely chopped
6 scallions, thinly sliced
1 large green bell pepper, coarsely chopped
3 to 4 fresh green chile peppers, coarsely chopped with seeds
5 jalapeño peppers, coarsely chopped with seeds
8 serrano peppers, coarsely chopped with seeds
¾ cup chopped fresh cilantro
½ cup red wine vinegar
¼ cup olive oil
½ tsp cayenne pepper
½ tsp freshly ground black pepper

Mix all ingredients in a large bowl and let sit for 30 minutes before serving.

Salsa Cruda

Makes about 1 cup

1 cup very ripe fresh tomatoes, coarsely chopped
2 Tbsp fresh lime juice
2 to 3 Tbsp finely chopped jalapeño or serrano chile peppers
1 small onion, coarsely chopped

Mix all the ingredients and let sit an hour. This sauce is best used within 6 hours; the longer it sits, the less intense and crunchy it becomes.

Serve with any type of barbecued food, fried shrimp and chicken or on grilled fish. It also makes a great dip for nachos or taco chips with guacamole.

Salsa Picante

Makes about 3 cups

4 large, ripe tomatoes, chopped
3 scallions, thinly sliced
2 Tbsp chopped fresh cilantro
2 ½ Tbsp fresh lime juice
2 fresh jalapeño or serranto chilies, trimmed and chopped (with seeds)
1 large clove garlic, chopped
½ cup water
Salt to taste

In a large bowl, mix the tomatoes, scallions, coriander and lime juice and set aside.

In a blender or food processor, blend the chilies and garlic until finely chopped. Add the water and process for another 2 to 3 seconds until well blended. Add the chile and garlic sauce to the tomato mixture and mix well; add salt to taste. Refrigerate until ready to serve.

Serve as a dip with taco chips and guacamole or as a condiment with tortillas, grilled meats and eggs. When freshly made it is VERY HOT, the longer it sits the more subdued its fire becomes. Serve within a few hours of making.

Or, if time doesn't allow, there are many excellent bottled salsas readily available at the super market.

Tortilla Chips

Store-bought chips are great, but, home-made are better if you have time to make them. Remember, you will want to make these well in advance of your party. Purchase corn tortillas, fresh or canned. Again, if you have the time you can really start from scratch and powder your own corn. In this case, purchase dried bulk corn and crush and then powder the corn with a pestle. If you do start from here, powder lots as you won't want to do this too often!

Take the powdered corn and make into a paste with water. You can add some spicing here, if you wish. Blend in some chili powder, paprika, white or cayenne pepper and salt to taste. If you have purchased pre-made tortillas, you can sprinkle these same spices on the full-size tortillas. You will require more, as this method is not as effective.

Fry the tortillas in a light oil until crispy. Tamp off oil and set to cool. Once cool, break up the tortillas into chips.

Serve with Salsa and a side dish of Guacamole Sauce.

Guacamole

1 avocado, mashed
Juice of ½ lemon
½ tomato, juiced, seeded,
and finely chopped
3 green onions, minced
Pinch of crushed dried red peppers
Dash Tabasco

Blend well together. Serve immediately or cover tightly with the avocado pit on top to prevent surface from darkening.

Chilled Raspberry Soup

Makes 6 - ½ cup servings

1 ½ cups fresh raspberries or 425 g container frozen unsweetened raspberries
1 cup (250 mL container) sour cream
¾ cup milk
Generous pinch of ground cardamom

Place fresh raspberries or entire contents of container of frozen raspberries and sour cream in a food processor. Whirl, using and on-and-off motion, until puréed.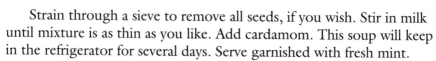

Strain through a sieve to remove all seeds, if you wish. Stir in milk until mixture is as thin as you like. Add cardamom. This soup will keep in the refrigerator for several days. Serve garnished with fresh mint.

Gazpacho Soup

Makes about 6 cups

2 large ripe tomatoes
1 large sweet pepper
1 garlic clove
½ cup fresh mixed herbs; chives, parsley, basil, chervil, tarragon
½ cup olive oil
3 Tbsp lemon or lime juice
3 cups chilled water or light stock
1 Spanish onion, thinly sliced
1 cup peeled, seeded, grated cucumber
1 tsp salt, or to taste
½ tsp paprika

Peel and seed the tomatoes and seed the sweet pepper. Chop along with the garlic clove and the herbs. Gradually add the olive oil, lemon or lime juice and the water or stock. Add the rest of the ingredients. If you prefer, use your blender to finely chop all ingredients. Chill the soup for at least 4 hours before serving.

To serve sprinkle each bowl with chopped parsley and bread crumbs.

The Salads

Traditional Caesar Salad

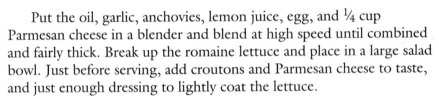

Use the Caesar dressing sparingly.

¼ cup oil
1 clove garlic, crushed
3 - 5 anchovies
2 - 3 Tbsp lemon juice
1 egg, raw or cooked gently for 60 - 90 seconds
¼ cup Parmesan cheese
1 head romaine lettuce, washed and dried
croutons
Parmesan cheese

Put the oil, garlic, anchovies, lemon juice, egg, and ¼ cup Parmesan cheese in a blender and blend at high speed until combined and fairly thick. Break up the romaine lettuce and place in a large salad bowl. Just before serving, add croutons and Parmesan cheese to taste, and just enough dressing to lightly coat the lettuce.

Spinach Salad

Serves 6 - 8

4 bunches of spinach
2 eggs, hard boiled
Vinegar, white wine to taste
3 - 4 strips of cooked bacon or bacon bits
Olive oil to taste
Cayenne pepper

Tenderly strip spinach leaves from root bases and clean. Spinach bruises easily, so be gentle. Rip into strips about ¾" wide and 3" long.

Chop egg and add to spinach with small pieces or bits of bacon. Refrigerate until ready to serve.

When ready to serve, drizzle a small amount of oil to very lightly coat spinach. Add a teaspoon or two of vinegar and a very light dusting of cayenne pepper to taste. Remember to keep out of sun or heat after preparation.

The Vegetables

Because this feast is very casual, light, quickly prepared vegetables are best. A vegetable tray featuring radishes, carrots, celery, cauliflower and cherry tomatoes offers a very colorful and tasty appetizer. An accompanying dip adds some zip.

Horseradish and Caper Dip

Makes 1 cup

½ cup sour cream
½ cup plain yogurt
2 Tbsp freshly grated horseradish, or 3 Tbsp drained bottled horseradish
2 Tbsp capers, drained
1 tsp Tabasco

Mix together all ingredients adding the Tabasco sauce to taste. Refrigerate and serve cold with raw vegetables.

Bleu Cheese Dip

Makes 2 ½ cups.

1 cup mayonnaise
2 Tbsp onion, finely chopped
1 Tbsp garlic powder
¼ cup parsley, finely chopped
½ cup sour cream
1 Tbsp fresh lemon juice
1 Tbsp white vinegar
¼ cup bleu cheese, crumbled
dash ground pepper
dash cayenne

Combine all ingredients and refrigerate for at least one hour before serving.

A couple of grilled vegetables (see Chart 3 - Outdoor Grill Timetable - Vegetables) is a welcome addition.

Big Ranch Barbecue

A full-bodied Cabernet Sauvignon or, for the adventurous, I'd even recommend a Zinfandel, served traditionally, as a Red.

This part of the feast will naturally take most of the time to prepare. The preparation time is fairly short but the cooking time is lengthy. This recipe works the best with a charcoal kettle-style barbecue. You can use gas, at a low setting.

Start by buying two or three beef briskets. It is best to order these in advance, as most butchers don't readily have these on hand. Get the thickest you can find. If the butcher has rolled the briskets, leave them that way for the start.

Prepare a bed of coals in a ring around the bottom of the barbecue, leaving the centre empty. Form a "tray" out of aluminum foil and place in the hole.

The basting sauce is made up of:

2 - 4 Tbsp olive oil
1 cup water
1 cup white wine
1 - 2 tsp Worcestershire sauce
2 Tbsp ketchup

Wipe down the briskets with chopped garlic and pepper. Start to cook over medium heat - sear the meat and turn often until outside of brisket is lightly seared. Pour some of the marinade into aluminum tray. Add wetted Hickory chips/shavings to coals. Heat should be kept low and chips added repeatedly so smoke is produced. Baste the brisket often and turn after basting, every few minutes.

Continue this process for about three hours. Keep a watch to ensure that the meat doesn't get dried out. If there is a sign of this early on; in first hour or so, the barbecue is too hot. Baste often and lower the heat. At approximately 3 hours, remove the aluminum tray. Do not discard.

For the dipping sauce:

½ cup water
½ cup dry white wine
2 Tbsp ketchup
1 tsp wine vinegar
1 tsp Worcestershire sauce

Place the tray in a frying pan or pot and turn on to medium-high heat. When hot, pour ½ cup water and ½ cup dry white wine into centre of the tray. Watch the steam that will be generated. Move the pan around to loosen all the drippings in the tray. Dump all of this into pan and scrape off any additional drippings from tray. Chips in the tray are okay in this mixture. Turn down to simmer and strain off solid materials. Add 2 Tbsp ketchup, 1 tsp wine vinegar and 1 tsp Worcestershire sauce. Reduce until the consistency of thick soup.

Remove the briskets from the barbecue and cut in strips across the grain.

Add dipping sauce and serve on Kaiser or hamburger buns. A bit of horseradish and/or a good mustard goes well with this.

A lemon or lime sorbet is excellent as a finishing touch.

Magician's Memos

Recipe changes, additions, & doodles!

Grilled Magic Recipes

Beef

Basic Barbecued Steak

Thick T-bone or Porterhouse steaks
Garlic powder or finely chopped garlic
Onion salt
Fresh black pepper

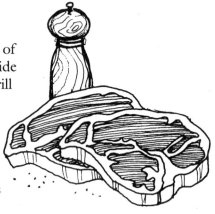

Cut off excess fat and notch side of steak to prevent curling. Dress one side of the steak and place that side on grill over a hot fire. Dress other side and flip. Quench fire by putting down hood on coal fires, or turn down to medium-low if gas or electric. Cook to desired doneness and remove from grill. Let stand 30 - 60 seconds and serve.

Blackened Sirloin

Makes 8 servings

1 Tbsp freshly ground white pepper
1 Tbsp freshly ground black pepper
1 Tbsp dry mustard
1 Tbsp paprika
2 tsp cayenne pepper
1 tsp dried fennel
½ tsp dried oregano
½ tsp dried thyme
⅓ cup butter
2 garlic cloves, minced
2 - 2 ½ lbs sirloin steak, about 1 ½" thick
1 Tbsp vegetable oil

Combine spices for seasoning mix. Set aside. Melt butter with garlic and place in a flat dish with a lip. When ready to cook steak, dip it into garlic butter. Then, pat seasoning mix into each side.

Preheat barbecue. Brush grill with oil. Steak will "blacken" so do not worry. The seasoning mix will create lots of smoke. This recipe is best served medium rare.

Remove from barbecue and let stand for 5 minutes. Thinly slice on the diagonal. Serve with rice and stir fry vegetables.

Steak with Pesto

Makes 4 servings

¼ cup soft butter
¼ cup pesto
2 Tbsp vegetable oil
1 large garlic clove, crushed
2 - 4 sirloin steaks, about 1 ½" thick
Freshly ground black pepper
1 large Spanish onion

Prepare pesto butter by stirring room-temperature butter with pesto. Refrigerate until fairly firm or ready to serve. Stir oil and garlic together. Set aside at room temperature.

Nick edges of steaks to prevent them curling. Roll in the black pepper and then baste well with the garlic mixture.

Place steak on greased grill about 4 inches above hot coals. Barbecue thickly sliced onion on grill with the steak, but only about half as long as the steak.

Serve with pesto butter, potatoes, and a light spinach salad.

Wine Steak

Makes 4 servings

4 New York strip or shell steaks (about 10 oz each)
⅓ cup vegetable oil
¼ cup dry red wine
3 green onions, chopped or 1 small onion, chopped (¼ cup)
Salt and pepper
Bearnaise Sauce
Stuffed Mushrooms

Trim excess fat from steaks, score remaining fat at 1" intervals around edge. Place in a large shallow utility dish. Combine oil, wine and shallots in a 1 cup measure; pour over steaks. Allow to marinate at room temperature at least 2 hours. Remove steaks from marinade. Reserve marinade.

Grill 4" from heat, brushing with marinade, 5 minutes on each side for rare, 10 minutes on each side for medium, and 15 minutes on each side for well done, or until done as you like.

Place steaks on carving board and season with salt and pepper. Allow steaks to "rest" 10 minutes. Serve with Bearnaise sauce and stuffed mushrooms.

Crumb-Coated Steak

Makes 8 servings

1 sirloin steak, cut 2" thick (about 4 lbs)
¼ cup prepared mustard
2 Tbsp vegetable oil
Crumb Topping (recipe follows)

Trim off any excess fat from steak, then score remaining fat edge every inch so meat will lie flat on grill.

Spread steak with mustard; let stand at room temperature 1 hour.

After grilling, brush steak all over with vegetable oil; pat Crumb Topping over top of meat and return to grill. Heat until crumbs are set.

Remove steak to a cutting board or large platter and garnish with red and green pepper rings.

Crumb Topping

Makes 3 cups. Place 6 slices white bread on a cookie sheet; toast in slow oven (300°F) 30 minutes, or until dry, crisp and richly golden; cool. Crush with rolling pin. Heat ¼ cup olive or vegetable oil with 1 tsp crumbled mixed Italian herbs in a medium saucepan; add bread crumbs; toss to mix well.

Herb-Basted Steak

Makes 6 servings.

1 cup dry red wine
¼ cup sliced green onion
¼ cup chopped green pepper
¼ cup chopped celery
¼ cup olive or vegetable oil
1 clove garlic, minced
1 tsp salt
1 flank steak (about 2 lbs)
1 bunch parsley, rosemary, or tarragon

Combine wine, green onion, green pepper, celery, olive oil, garlic and salt in a small saucepan. Bring to boiling; reduce heat and cover. Simmer 15 minutes and cool completely.

Place flank steak in a glass dish and pour cooled marinade over meat. Marinate at least 1 hour at room temperature.

Tie a large bunch of washed parsley, rosemary or tarragon with string. Pour marinade from steak into a bowl.

Grill, 4" from heat, basting with reserved marinade, using parsley, rosemary or tarragon bunch as a basting brush. Carve on the diagonal into thin slices and serve with garlic bread and baked potato.

Oriental Grilled Steaks

Makes 4 servings

4 individual top round steaks, cut 1" thick (about 3 lbs)
½ cup soy sauce
½ cup dry sherry
2 Tbsp sugar
½ tsp powdered ginger
¼ tsp dry mustard
½ tsp garlic powder

Place steaks in plastic bag or shallow glass dish. Combine soy sauce, sherry, sugar, ginger, dry mustard and garlic powder in a 2 cup measure; pour marinade over steaks. Turn steaks to coat all sides and seal bag or cover dish with plastic wrap.

Marinate in refrigerator 4 to 6 hours. Let stand at room temperature 1 hour. Remove from marinade and reserve marinade.

Grill, 4" from heat, 5 minutes for rare, 7 minutes for medium and 10 minutes for well done; brush with remaining marinade; turn with tongs.

Steak au Poivre

Serve steak, French-style, with its thick coating of cracked pepper.

Makes 6 to 8 servings

1 sirloin steak, 2" thick (about 4 lbs)
4 to 8 Tbsp cracked pepper
Salt
¼ cup brandy

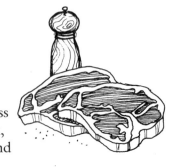

Wipe steak with damp paper towels. Press half of the pepper into each side of the steak, using your fingers and heal of hand. Let stand at room temperature for 1 hour.

Grill and sprinkle with salt when removed from heat.

Transfer the steak to a hot sizzle-platter. Warm brandy in a small metal saucepan with flameproof handle over grill; pour over steak; ignite, using long fireplace matches. Serve.

Grilled Sirloin Steak

Makes 8 servings

1 sirloin steak, cut 2" thick (about 4 lbs)
⅔ cup olive or vegetable oil
⅓ cup wine or cider vinegar
1 tsp salt
1 tsp dried thyme, crumbled
¼ tsp pepper

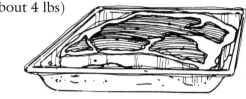

Remove steak from refrigerator 2 hours before cooking. Trim off any excess fat, then score remaining fat edge at 1" intervals so meat will lie flat on grill. Place steak in a shallow glass dish.

Mix oil, vinegar, salt, thyme and pepper in a small bowl; pour over steak; cover with plastic wrap. Let stand at room temperature 2 hours.

Grill, 5" from heat, brushing several times with marinade from pan.

Remove steak to a cutting board or large platter; let "rest" 15 minutes before slicing. Slice steak ¼" thick.

Garlic-Grilled Steak

Makes 3 servings

3 rib eye steaks, cut 2" thick (about 1 lb each)
¼ cup vegetable oil
1 chopped garlic clove
Bleu Cheese Butter (recipe follows)
salt and pepper

Trim excess fat from steaks and score remaining fat at 1" intervals. Allow to stand at room temperature about 1 hour before barbecuing.

Combine oil and garlic in a cup and allow to stand with steak.

Coat steak generously with garlic oil on both sides. Remove steak to platter; top with Bleu Cheese Butter and sprinkle with salt and pepper.

Bleu Cheese Butter

This tangy butter enhances the flavor of the burgers and steaks and can be used for other meats as well.

Makes ¾ cup

½ cup bleu or Roquefort cheese
¼ cup butter or margarine, softened
2 Tbsp sherry, white wine, brandy or cream

Remove cheese and butter or margarine from refrigerator. Crumble the cheese. Allow both to stand at room temperature about 1 hour.

Mash cheese with butter in a small bowl with a fork. Stir in sherry, wine, brandy, or cream and mix to a smooth paste. Turn into a bowl.

Serve at room temperature on beef of all kinds or chicken breasts.

Rosemary Steak

Makes 8 servings

1 chuck steak, cut 2" thick (about 4 lbs)
Vegetable oil
2 Tbsp butter or margarine
2 Tbsp chopped chives
2 Tbsp rosemary, crumbled

Remove steak from refrigerator 1 hour before grilling. Trim off any excess fat, then score remaining fat edge at 1" intervals so meat will lie flat on grill and not curl during cooking. Brush steak all over with vegetable oil; pat rosemary onto both sides. Let stand at room temperature 1 hour. Grill until steak is done as you like it. Remove to a cutting board and dot with butter or margarine; let melt into steak and sprinkle with chives. Slice steak into ¼" thick slices. Serve with a green vegetable and salad.

Hawaiian Beef Teriyaki

Makes 4 servings

2 lbs boneless beef steak
1 ¾ cup soy sauce
½ cup sugar
½ tsp crushed garlic
1 Tbsp grated fresh ginger or 2 Tbsp minced preserved ginger

Cut meat into 4 pieces and place in a bowl. In a pan combine the soy, sugar, garlic, and ginger. Heat just until sugar is dissolved then cool.

Pour mixture over meat and marinate for 1 hour or longer. Remove meat from marinade and grill over glowing coals.

Slice each steak into finger-sized pieces and serve one steak to a customer.

Flavor Variations for Beef Teriyaki: Add to the marinade given above any one of these: 1 Tbsp sake (Japanese rice wine) or sauterne, or 1 Tbsp chili sauce or ketchup. Serve with rice.

Barbecued Burgers

This is your basic burger recipe. Use your imagination when preparing these for your family and friends.

¼ lb ground beef per burger
finely chopped garlic or garlic powder
finely chopped onion
pepper and salt
medium cheddar cheese

A leaner beef will not flare up as much as regular ground beef. Form patties by making firm ¼ pound balls and then flatten using palm of hand. Sprinkle with above ingredients and place over a hot fire to sear. Turn burgers and place slice of cheese on top. Then douse fire by replacing top of a coal barbecue, or turning down a gas or electric barbecue. When cooked to your taste, serve on warmed buns.

Toppings can include sliced raw or cooked onion, ketchup, mustard, relish. Pickles, tomatoes and lettuce are also good. Fried or raw mushrooms, bacon and peppers are also good. Chuckwagon Ranch Sauce used as a baste is a nice addition.

Chuckwagon Ranch Sauce

Makes approximately 4 cups

3 cups (24 oz) tomato sauce
⅔ cup brown sugar
½ cup ketchup
⅓ cup vinegar
4 Tbsp dry prepared mustard
1 cup chopped onion
2 chopped garlic cloves
3 Tbsp chili powder

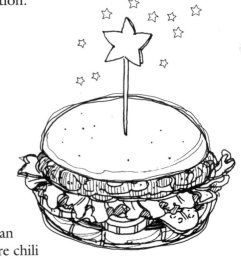

Combine all ingredients in a pan and let simmer for 5 minutes. More chili powder can be added to make "hotter".
Can be used as a marinade or a baste for all kinds of barbecued meats.

Caesar Burgers

Makes 4 servings

1 egg
¼ cup Caesar salad dressing
1 large garlic clove, crushed, or ¼ tsp garlic powder
¼ tsp freshly ground black pepper or cayenne pepper
½ cup freshly grated Parmesan cheese
1 lb ground beef

Whisk egg, salad dressing, anchovy paste, garlic and pepper in a medium-size bowl. Stir in bread crumbs and Parmesan. Add ground beef and work in with a fork or your hands until thoroughly blended.

Shape mixture into 4 patties, each about 4" wide and ¾" thick. Place on a greased grill about 4" from hot coals. Barbecue for 5 minutes per side for medium-rare patties.

Swiss Peppercorn

Makes 4 servings

1 egg
1 Tbsp green peppercorns or capers, rinsed and drained
Freshly ground black pepper
1 lb ground beef
¾ cup chopped or cubed Gruyere or Swiss cheese

Whisk egg in a large bowl. Stir in peppercorns and a generous pinch of ground pepper until blended. Add meat and sprinkle with Gruyere and bread crumbs. Work with your hands or a fork until blended.

Shape into 4 patties, each about 4" wide and ¾" thick. Place on a greased grill about 4" from hot coals. Barbecue for 5 minutes per side for medium-rare patties.

Feta Burgers

Makes 4 servings

¾ cup crumbled feta cheese
1 egg
½ tsp Italian seasoning
¼ tsp salt
Freshly ground black pepper
1 lb ground beef

Place cheese in a large bowl and crumble with a fork. Add egg and seasonings and stir together until blended. Add meat and work with your hands or a fork until blended.

Shape into 4 patties, each about 4" wide and ¾" thick. Place on greased grill about 4" from hot coals. Barbecue 5 minutes per side for medium-rare burgers.

Serve with Fresh Greek Salad (see "Accompaniments").

Peppered Burgers

Makes 4 servings

1 egg
1 garlic clove, crushed
¼ tsp Worcestershire sauce
⅛ tsp Tabasco sauce
¼ tsp salt
¼ tsp freshly ground black pepper
3 whole green onions, chopped
1 lb ground beef

Blend egg, garlic, Worcestershire, Tabasco and other seasonings into a large bowl. Stir in onions. Add meat and work with your hands or a fork until evenly blended.

Shape into 4 patties, each about 4" wide and ¾" thick. Place on greased grill about 4" from hot coals. Barbecue 5 minutes per side for medium-rare burgers.

Serve on thick slices of crusty French bread with sliced tomatoes along with a Caesar salad.

Surf 'N' Turf Kebabs

Makes 4 servings

½ cup vegetable oil
2 Tbsp freshly squeezed lime juice
2 Tbsp freshly squeezed lemon juice
2 garlic cloves, crushed
2 Tbsp finely minced fresh ginger
½ lb beef tenderloin or sirloin, in 1 ½" cubes
24 medium to large shrimp or prawns, shelled and de-veined

Preheat barbecue. Whisk oil with lime and lemon juice, garlic and ginger. Set aside.

Place meat and shrimp in oil mixture and stir until coated. Marinate in fridge for 1 to 2 hours.

Thread meat on metal skewers alternately with whole shrimp or prawns. Brush with oil mixture. Place on greased grill over medium-hot coals, about 4" above heat. Baste often while cooking. Watch when you remove – the skewers will be hot.

Serve with rice and a potato salad or a green salad.

Beef and Veggie Kebabs

Makes 6 servings

2 lb beef sirloin tip, cubed
1 cup Italian salad dressing
1 tsp dried oregano, crumbled
1 small eggplant, cut into cubes
2 medium zucchini, cut into slices
2 white onions, cut into chunks

Place beef in a glass dish with Italian dressing and oregano; toss well; cover with plastic wrap. Then refrigerate at least 2 hours; then let stand at room temperature 1 hour.

Place eggplant, zucchini and white onions in separate piles in a large skillet; pour in boiling water to a depth of 1". Bring to boiling; lower heat; simmer 5 minutes; drain.

Remove beef from dish; reserve marinade. Thread meat alternately with vegetables on 6 long skewers; brush with marinade.

Grill, 4" from heat, turning and basting with marinade, 10 minutes for rare, 12 minutes for medium and 15 minutes for well done.

Okanagan Barbecue

Makes 6 servings

3 lbs top sirloin or chuck steak
2 tsp salt
1 cup peach jam
½ cup lemon juice
1 Tbsp Worcestershire sauce
2 large oranges
2 fresh peaches
2 Tbsp chutney

Trim beef and cut into 1½" cubes; sprinkle with salt; place in a large glass or ceramic dish. Combine peach jam, chutney, lemon juice and Worcestershire sauce in a bowl until smooth; pour over beef; cover with plastic wrap; refrigerate 2 hours.

Drain marinade from beef and reserve. Cut oranges and peaches into wedges. Alternate beef and orange and peach wedges on 12 long skewers.

Grill, 4" from heat, basting and turning kebabs several times, 10 minutes for rare, 13 for medium and 16 for well done beef.

Beef Kebabs

Makes 4 servings

2 lbs beef chuck, cut in 1 ½" pieces
1 green pepper, cut in 1" pieces
1 tomato, cut in wedges
1 medium onion, cut in wedges
½ lb mushrooms

Alternate meat pieces with vegetables on eight 8" skewers. Place on grill; brush with Caribbean Barbecue Sauce.

Grill about 20 minutes, turning over once. Continue to brush with sauce during grilling. Serve with hot, cooked rice.

Caribbean Barbecue Sauce

Makes ¾ cup

½ cup table molasses
¼ cup prepared mustard
3 Tbsp vinegar
2 Tbsp Worcestershire sauce
½ tsp Tabasco
1 tsp ground ginger
2 Tbsp soy sauce

Blend molasses and mustard. Add remaining ingredients; mix well.

Sassy Sauced Brisket

Makes 8 servings

2 lbs uncooked beef brisket
½ cup chili sauce
2 Tbsp vegetable oil
1 tsp horseradish
⅛ tsp Tabasco sauce
Pinch garlic powder

Tie beef brisket in a compact shape. Place in a large saucepan and cover with hot water. Bring to a boil. Periodically skim foam from water. Cover, reduce heat and simmer until meat is very tender, about 2 to 2 ½ hours.

When ready to barbecue, preheat coals. Whisk remaining ingredients together. Slice brisket into ½" slices. Place on greased grill at least 4" from hot coals. Baste with chili sauce mixture and grill, turning and basting frequently, until meat is piping hot, about 8 minutes. (See FEASTING for full menu.)

Shirley's Maui Ribs

Makes 4 servings

1 Tbsp sugar
1 Tbsp minced garlic
1 tsp vegetable oil
⅜ cup soy sauce
½ tsp pepper
1 Tbsp honey
¼ cup minced green onion
¼ tsp powdered ginger
⅛ cup sherry
4 lb short ribs

Combine first 9 ingredients in bowl large enough to hold all the ribs. Butterfly ribs if bones are longer than 1". Marinate for a minimum of overnight, longer if possible, turning or stirring occasionally. Barbecue or broil 3 to 5 minutes per side.

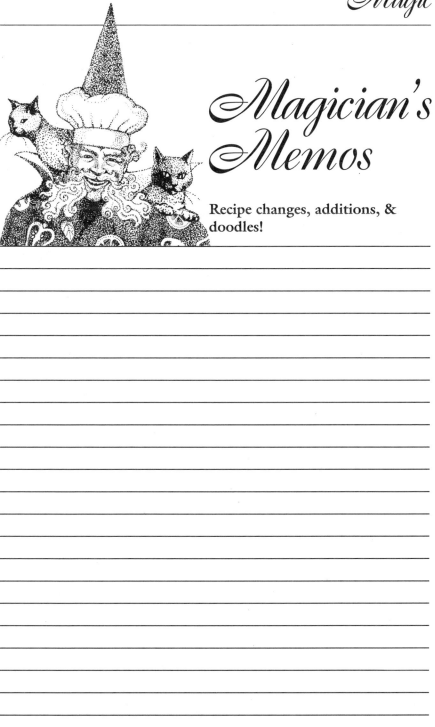

Magician's Memos

Recipe changes, additions, & doodles!

Poultry

Chicken Brochettes

Makes 6 servings

2 cup yogurt
Juice from 2 limes
3 garlic cloves, crushed
2 Tbsp chopped fresh ginger
1 Tbsp ground cumin
1 Tbsp ground coriander
3 ½ lbs chicken pieces
1 large Bermuda onion

In a large bowl, stir yogurt with lime juice, garlic, chopped fresh ginger, cumin and coriander. Skin and bone chicken. Then, cut into 1 ½" cubes.

Stir chicken pieces into yogurt mixture. Cover and refrigerate overnight, stirring occasionally.

When ready to grill, oil the grill, preheat barbecue and place grill about 4" above coals.

Cut onion into wedges and place on metal skewers alternating with pieces of chicken. Grill over hot coals about 5 minutes per side.

Vegetable alternative: In place of the Bermuda onion, use squares of red pepper and 1" pieces of green onion.

Watch the skewers, they'll be hot. Serve with carrots, rice and coleslaw.

Rosemary Chicken

Makes 4 to 6 servings

½ cup vegetable oil
Freshly squeezed juice from 1 lemon
2 tsp liquid honey
2 garlic cloves, crushed
½ tsp dried thyme
1 tsp dried rosemary, crushed, or 1 Tbsp chopped fresh rosemary
Salt and freshly ground black pepper
3 ½ lb roasting chicken or 6 chicken breasts or legs

Combine oil, juice, honey, garlic and seasonings in a wide shallow bowl. Blend well.

Cut roasting chicken into serving size pieces. Place skin-side down in oil mixture. Cover and refrigerate 3 hours, turning once.

Place on aluminum foil on top of barbecue grill. Watch for flare-ups. Keep heat constant but low so chicken won't burn. Turn often. Do not baste until ¾ cooked, then baste regularly.

Sweet & Sour Chicken Legs

Makes 8 servings.

1 cup pineapple juice
¼ cup honey
¼ cup lemon juice
1 Tbsp soy sauce
1 Tbsp Worcestershire sauce
1 clove garlic, minced
2 tsp salt
1 tsp dried basil, crumbled
1 tsp dry mustard
¼ tsp bottled red pepper seasoning
8 broiler-fryer legs or quarters (about 3 lbs)

Combine pineapple juice, honey, lemon juice, soy sauce, Worcestershire sauce, garlic, salt, basil, mustard and red pepper seasoning in a large jar with screw top. Shake to blend well. Refrigerate for at least 2 hours to blend flavors before using as a marinade.

Grill chicken pieces, skin side down, 6" from heat, turning pieces with tongs several times for 30 minutes.

Brush chicken with above marinade and grill, turning and basting several times, 20 minutes longer, or until chicken is tender and well glazed. Watch flare-ups and quench them carefully. The glaze will burn if you aren't careful here.

Chicken Kebabs

Makes 4 servings

2 lbs boneless, skinned chicken breast, cut into 1" wide strips
2 Tbsp olive oil
2 Tbsp white wine vinegar
2 Tbsp chopped fresh parsley
1 Tbsp chopped fresh basil or 1 tsp dried basil, crumbled
1 large zucchini, trimmed and sliced
1 red pepper, seeded and cut into chunks
12 mushrooms

Combine the chicken with oil, vinegar, parsley and basil in a bowl. Marinate for 1 hour at room temperature, or cover and refrigerate overnight. Drain, reserving the marinade. Thread chicken with zucchini, red pepper and mushrooms on skewers. Brush with reserved marinade. Grill, brushing with marinade, until chicken is cooked through and vegetables are tender.

Chicken Breasts Milano

Makes 8 servings

8 whole chicken breasts, split (about 10 oz each)
½ cup olive oil
½ cup dry white wine
2 cloves garlic, crushed
1 Tbsp chopped parsley
1 tsp dried oregano, crumbled
Salt and pepper
⅛ to ¼ tsp crushed red pepper flakes
⅓ cup grated Parmesan cheese

Steamed spinach leaves
Hot cooked rice
Red pepper strips

Marinate chicken breast halves in a mixture of oil, wine, garlic, parsley, oregano, salt and pepper to taste and red pepper flakes in a shallow pan; cover and refrigerate several hours, or overnight. Remove from fridge and let sit at least 2 hours before cooking time. Remove from marinade, reserving marinade.

Place breast halves, skin-side up, in one or two roasting pans. Brush with part of the reserved marinade. Barbecue on aluminium foil, skin side down for 10 to 15 minutes, or bake in a moderate oven (375°F) basting occasionally with marinade, 40 minutes, or until skin is crisp. Sprinkle part of Parmesan over chicken and return to barbecue without aluminum foil, turn often until cooked watching flare-ups.

Line a platter with spinach, then rice. Arrange chicken breast halves on top. Sprinkle with additional Parmesan and garnish with red pepper strips.

Pepper-Lemon Chicken

Makes 4 servings

½ tsp coarsely ground fresh black pepper
Finely grated peel and juice from 1 lemon
¼ cup vegetable oil
4 chicken breasts, skinned and boned

Combine pepper, lemon peel, 2 Tbsp juice and vegetable oil in a medium-size bowl. Whisk together until evenly blended.

Immerse chicken breasts in mixture, then place on grill about 4" from hot coals. Grill, while turning and basting frequently with the lemon mixture, until the chicken is tender, about 15 to 18 minutes.

For more flavor, immerse boned breasts in basting mixture, leave refrigerated for 1 to 2 hours. Then grill as above.

Western Barbecued Turkey

Makes 4 to 6 servings

1 turkey (4 to 6 lbs) cut in pieces for serving
1 cup ketchup
1 ¼ cups water
½ cup red wine
1 Tbsp wine vinegar
½ cup butter
½ cup onion, finely chopped
1 - 3 garlic cloves, finely chopped
2 tsp Worcestershire sauce
1 Tbsp sugar
2 tsp paprika
½ tsp salt

Combine all ingredients, except turkey, in a pot and heat to a boil. Brush the turkey with the hot sauce and place skin side down on the grill. Cook 1 hour, basting frequently with the sauce. Turn skin side up and continue cooking for about ¾ to 1 ¼ hours, or until turkey is tender, basting frequently. (Remember: slow cooking is essential to success!!)

For cooking in an oven, place turkey, skin side down, in a roasting pan. Combine remaining ingredients and heat to boiling then pour over turkey. Cover and bake in a moderately hot oven (375°F) for 1 hour, basting turkey occasionally. Remove cover and turn turkey skin side up. Continue baking, uncovered, for about ¾ to 1 ¼ hours, or until turkey is tender, basting and turning turkey occasionally.

If sauce becomes too thick during cooking, add a little more wine or water.

Magician's Memos

Recipe changes, additions, & doodles!

Pork & Ham

Polish Loin of Pork

Makes 8 servings

1 centre-cut pork loin (about 6 lbs) or
1 boneless pork loin roast
(about 4 lbs)
1 bottle (750 mL) cocktail sherry
1 medium onion, quartered and
studded with 4 cloves
2 - 3" pieces stick cinnamon
4 peppercorns
1 box (8 oz) pitted prunes
1 box (8 oz) dried apricots
2 or 3 lemon slices
Red and green cabbage wedges

Remove meat from pork rib bones; use bones as spareribs at another barbecue. Trim excess fat from roast. Tie roast into a compact cylinder by wrapping with strong cotton twine (never thread) at 2" intervals, securing with snug butcher or square knots. Place in large plastic bag in utility dish. Add 2 cups of the sherry, onion quarters studded with cloves, 1 of the cinnamon sticks and peppercorns. Tie bag securely; turn bag several times to coat meat evenly. Marinate at room temperature 2 hours, or refrigerate overnight. Let meat stand at room temperature 1 hour before grilling; drain and reserve marinade.

Meanwhile, rinse prunes and apricots under running water; place in medium saucepan; add remaining sherry, cinnamon sticks and lemon slices. Bring to boiling; lower heat; simmer 30 minutes, or until tender. Build a medium fire in a kettle grill or set gas or electric grill to medium. Place a foil pan in centre of coals to collect drippings. Grill, basting with marinade several times, 1 hour, 50 minutes, or until a meat thermometer inserted in centre registers 170° F. Remove to a heated platter and allow to "rest" 20 minutes. Serve with the dried fruit mixture and red and green cabbage wedges, steamed in foil or simmered in boiling water in a large saucepan on the edge of the grill.

Sweet & Sour Ham Steak

Makes 6 servings

1 centre-cut ham steak, cut 1 ½" thick (about 2 lbs)
½ cup firmly packed brown sugar
⅓ cup beer or apple juice
2 Tbsp prepared hot mustard
1 tsp pumpkin pie spice

Trim excess fat from steak; score remaining fat at 1" intervals.

Grill, turning once, about 10 minutes.

While ham steak grills, combine sugar, beer or apple juice, mustard and pumpkin pie spice in a small metal saucepan with a flameproof handle. Heat on grill, stirring several times, until bubbly-hot.

Baste the ham steak with beer mixture; grill 5 minutes, turn and baste again; grill 5 minutes longer, or until well glazed.

Pork with Sage

Makes 4 servings

1 lb ground pork
1 egg
Finely grated peel of 1 orange
¼ tsp dry mustard
2 Tbsp finely chopped fresh sage or 1 tsp dried sage
½ tsp salt
Freshly ground black pepper or generous pinch of cayenne pepper
¼ cup fine dry bread crumbs

Whisk egg in a medium-size bowl. Stir in orange peel, mustard and seasonings. Add meat. Evenly sprinkle with bread crumbs. Work with your hands until blended.

Shape into 4 patties, each about 4" wide and ¾" thick. Place on a greased grill 4" from hot coals. Barbecue for 6 minutes per side.

Serve pork patties with a sauce made by blending a little sour cream with Dijon mustard. Serve along with a crisp coleslaw.

Garlic & Herbed Ribs

Makes 6 servings

2 racks of spare ribs, approximately 3 lbs
½ cup white wine
½ cup vegetable oil
2 Tbsp ketchup
2 Tbsp brown sugar
½ tsp Worcestershire sauce
4 garlic cloves, crushed
2 tsp dried basil, crumbled
1 tsp dried oregano, crumbled, or ½ tsp ground oregano

Trim excess fat from ribs. Cut ribs into 4" pieces. To ensure tender ribs, place in a large saucepan. Fill with enough water to cover completely. Bring to a boil, then cover and simmer for 1 hour.

As soon as ribs are tender, drain well and, while still hot, place in a dish. Whisk the marinade ingredients together and pour over the ribs. Refrigerate, keeping ribs immersed in liquid for at least 4 hours or preferably overnight. Turn the ribs several times.

When ready to grill, bring ribs to room temperature before barbecuing. Place ribs on preheated grill at least 4" from hot coals. Generously brush with sauce mixture. Grill for about 5 minutes. Turn and baste again. Continue basting and turning until meat is golden-brown, about 10 minutes. Watch for flare-ups, especially with the sugar content of this recipe.

Ham with Basil Mustard

Makes 4 servings

2 to 4 precooked ham steaks, about ½" thick
2 Tbsp prepared or Dijon mustard
2 Tbsp vegetable oil
¼ cup finely chopped fresh basil or 1 ½ tsp dried basil

Whisk mustard with oil and basil. Place ham steaks on a preheated greased grill about 4" from hot coals. Generously brush with mustard mixture. Barbecue about 8 to 10 minutes or until piping hot, turning frequently and brushing with marinade.

Barbecued Spareribs

Yields 4 servings

4 lb spareribs

Sauce:

¾ cup Madeira wine
2 garlic cloves
1 tsp salt
1 tsp black pepper
2 Tbsp sugar
2 tsp chili powder
1 cup wine vinegar
¼ tsp Tabasco sauce
¼ cup vegetable oil
2 onions, minced
½ cup tomato purée
1 - 14 oz can tomatoes
1 tsp dried mustard
1 tsp thyme
1 large green pepper, diced

To shorten cooking time, precook ribs in water with salt and vinegar added, for about an hour. Drain, pat dry, then place on grill for about 20 - 30 minutes and brush with the sauce.

For the sauce: Combine Madeira wine with garlic; marinate 4 lbs of meaty spareribs in the refrigerator overnight - cut into 2 x 2" chunks. Mix the rest of the ingredients in a saucepan, and bring to a boil, then simmer for 15 minutes, stirring occasionally. Brush on the spareribs frequently as they finish cooking. Watch for flare-ups on the barbecue as there is sugar in this recipe.

Honey-Barbecued Ribs

Makes 3 - 4 servings

3 lbs lean ribs, cut into 2 x 2" pieces
¼ cup soy sauce
4 Tbsp honey
2 Tbsp sugar
1 tsp salt
1 cup chicken stock
1 Tbsp vegetable oil
Pinch of cayenne

Cook ribs in boiling water until tender. Drain. Mix remaining ingredients and soak ribs in refrigerator in this mixture for 1 hour.

Drain and place ribs on grill, about 4" from coals. Turn and baste with the marinade, about 15 to 20 minutes.

Makes 4 servings. Serve with Hot Mustard Sauce made by mixing dry mustard with enough water to make a runny sauce.

Pineapple Spareribs

Makes 4 servings.

5 lbs spareribs
2 cloves garlic
1 Tbsp salt
1 tsp oregano
½ tsp freshly-ground black pepper
4 garlic cloves, crushed
4 cups pineapple juice
1 lb liquid honey

Cook ribs in water to cover and add the seasonings. Cook until tender. Remove ribs and cool liquid. Skim off any fat. Add 4 crushed garlic cloves and pineapple juice.

Soak ribs in this marinade in refrigerator overnight. Drain. Grill about 4" from coals brushing with honey to make a glaze for about 15 to 20 minutes. Serve with mustard mixed with orange marmalade for a real taste treat.

Barbecued Spare Ribs

Makes 4 servings

3 to 4 lbs ribs
1 lemon thinly sliced
1 large onion thinly sliced
1 cup ketchup
⅓ cup Worcestershire sauce
1 tsp chili powder
¼ tsp salt
Dash of Tabasco
2 cup water

Arrange ribs in long strips in a shallow baking pan, fat side down. Arrange slices of lemon and onion on meat and roast at 450° F for half an hour.

Combine remaining ingredients and bring to boiling point in a saucepan. Pour sauce, little by little, over ribs and reduce heat to 350° F, and bake till tender, about an hour. Place over coals and cook for 15 minutes turning frequently.

Magician's Memos

Recipe changes, additions, & doodles!

Lamb

Grilled Lamb Steaks

Ask your butcher to cut steaks from a leg of lamb, or use thick shoulder chops.

Makes 4 servings

4 lamb steaks, cut 1" thick
(about 2 lbs)
Salt and pepper
¼ cup butter or margarine,
softened
2 Tbsp chopped fresh mint

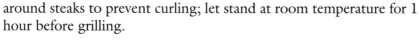

Trim excess fat from lamb, score remaining fat around steaks to prevent curling; let stand at room temperature for 1 hour before grilling.

Grill lamb, 5" from heat, for 10 minutes; turn and grill 10 minutes longer. Sprinkle salt and pepper over chops and place on a heated platter.

Combine butter or margarine and mint in a small bowl; spread over steaks and serve very hot.

Lamb Greek Style

Makes 4 servings

12 lamb chops
¼ cup olive oil
¼ cup lemon juice
2 to 4 cloves garlic, halved
Salt and pepper to taste
1 ½ tsp dried oregano, crumbled

Place lamb in a large plastic or glass bowl. Combine oil, lemon juice, garlic, salt, pepper and oregano in cup. Pour mixture over lamb and blend into meat, marinate at least 6 hours. Barbecue until done as desired.

Barbecued Lamb Leg

Makes 6 - 8 Servings

4 - 6 lb leg of lamb
4 - 8 cloves garlic

Cut small pockets in meat and insert quartered garlic cloves. Use garlic according to your like of garlic (the more you like, the more you use).

Marinade:

⅓ cup olive oil
⅓ cup white wine
3 chopped garlic cloves
4 Tbsp Dijon mustard
3 sprigs fresh rosemary
2 pinches each of thyme and oregano
1 Tbsp honey

Warm all marinade ingredients in microwave at high for 45 seconds before using.

For kettle or charcoal-type barbecues, start medium hot and then tone down - remember, the fats in lamb break down slowly so watch for flare-ups. With gas, medium-low heat is good. Watch carefully for flare-ups. Turn often as outer meat sears. Generously baste with marinade on every turn or baste with marinade regularly if using a rotisserie.

Meat is ready when clear liquids start to stop running freely – 45 - 90 minutes after starting. Let stand 15 minutes before cutting. A "little" pink is good.

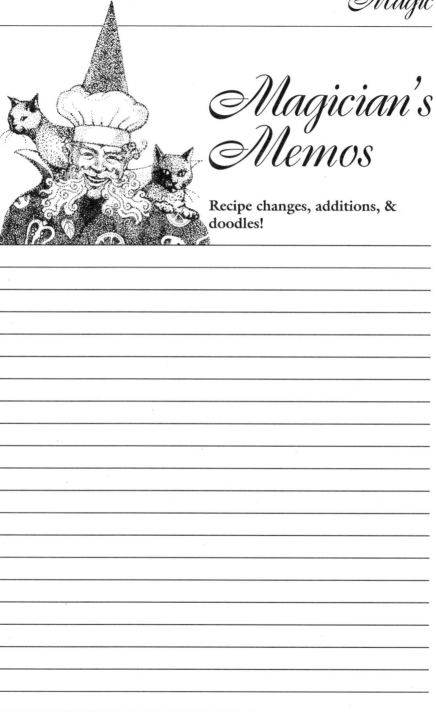

GRILLED
Magic

Magician's Memos

Recipe changes, additions, & doodles!

Other Meats

Barbecued Hot Dogs

Wieners, Sausages or other rolled meat
Bacon
Toppings
Buns

Diagonally score your meat so it doesn't explode. Baste with a tomato-based sauce and grill over a medium fire or heat. Bacon may be wrapped around wieners before cooking. Serve with traditional toppings including ketchup, mustard, relish, chopped onions and chopped tomatoes.

Barbecued Italian Sausage

Makes 8 servings

2 lb sweet Italian sausages
Beer Baste (recipe follows)
2 packages (8 buns each) hot dog buns, toasted
3 jars (6 oz each) marinated artichoke hearts, drained

Diagonally cut Italian sausages about ⅛" deep with paring knife.

Grill, 6" from heat, turning often, for 8 to 10 minutes; brush with Beer Baste and grill and baste 10 minutes longer (watch for flare-ups). Serve on hot dog buns with artichoke hearts and light mustard.

Beer Baste

Makes about 1 ¾ cups

1 cup bottled barbecue sauce
¾ cup beer
1 Tbsp Worcestershire sauce

Combine barbecue sauce, beer, and Worcestershire sauce in a 2 cup jar and refrigerate overnight before using.

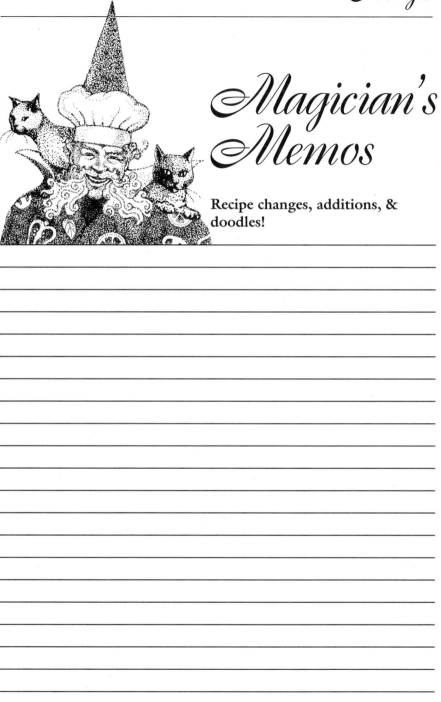

Magician's Memos

Recipe changes, additions, & doodles!

Fish & Seafood

Grilled Whole Salmon

Makes 8 servings

Whole salmon
Freshly ground white pepper
Small bunch fresh dill
Vegetable oil
Lemon slices

Allow ¼ to ½ pound per person. Sprinkle cavity of salmon with white pepper. Fill with sprigs of fresh dill if you wish or thin slices of lemon. Brush outside of salmon with vegetable oil.

Measure thickness (not length) of salmon at its thickest part. A 6 pound (3 kg) whole salmon will measure about 2 ½ to 3" thick. Allow 10 to 15 minutes grilling time for each inch of thickness.

Place fish in a greased fish basket and sit it about 4" above hot coals. If you do not have a basket, place fish on a greased grill about 4" above hot coals.

Keep lid of barbecue closed or cover fish with a loose tent of heavy foil. Barbecue for 15 to 20 minutes on each side, turning only once midway through grilling. Place a dab of dilled butter on each serving.

See "Feasting" for full salmon dinner menu.

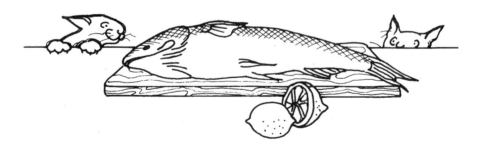

Seafood Kebabs

Makes 6 servings

2 doz sea scallops
2 doz shrimp, shelled and de-veined
2 Tbsp olive or vegetable oil
2 Tbsp fresh lime juice
1 Tbsp prepared Dijon mustard
1 Spanish or mild onion
1 lime, cut into thin wedges
1 pint cherry tomatoes, stemmed

Marinate scallops and shrimp in mixture of oil, lime juice and mustard in a large bowl, 1 hour at room temperature. Drain, reserving marinade. Thread the seafood with onion slices, lime wedges and tomatoes on 12 skewers. Brush with marinade. Grill, brushing with marinade until seafood is cooked.

Mustard Grilled Salmon

Makes 6 servings

6 salmon steaks (8 oz each)
⅛ cup vegetable oil
¼ cup dry white wine
⅜ cup lemon juice
3 Tbsp Dijon mustard
¼ cup onion, chopped
½ clove garlic, minced
Salt and pepper to taste

Place salmon steaks in a single layer in large glass utility dish.

Combine oil with wine, lemon juice, mustard, chopped onion, garlic, salt and pepper in small bowl, blending well. Pour over salmon; turn steaks in mustard mixture to coat well. Refrigerate 3 hours, turning once.

Drain salmon, reserving marinade. Place salmon on grill; brush with reserved marinade.

Grill salmon, 4" from heat, 5 minutes; turn; brush with marinade; grill 5 minutes or until fish flakes.

Salmon with Rosemary & Lemon

Makes 12 servings

1 whole salmon, dressed and boned (about 6 lbs)
1 lemon, thinly sliced
5 sprigs fresh rosemary or 2 Tbsp dried rosemary, crumbled
1 cup lemon juice
1 cup butter or margarine
1 tsp salt, or to taste
¼ tsp pepper

Build a medium fire, or set gas or electric grill to medium. Rinse fish in cold water; pat dry with paper towels. Place lemon slices and the 5 sprigs of rosemary or dried rosemary in the fish cavity. Combine lemon juice, butter or margarine, salt and pepper in a small saucepan with a flameproof handle on the grill; heat until butter melts. Brush fish with lemon butter; place in a fish grilling rack, if available. Grill, 6" from heat, turning and basting with lemon butter several times, 20 to 40 minutes, or until fish flakes easily. Carefully place on a heated fish platter.

Stuffed Red Snapper

Makes 6 servings

1 whole red snapper, cleaned and scaled (about 3 lbs)
¼ cup butter or margarine
¼ cup onion, chopped
1 package (10 oz) fresh spinach, well washed, stemmed and chopped
½ cup dry white wine
2 cups soft white bread cubes (4 slices)
½ tsp salt, or to taste
⅛ tsp freshly ground pepper
Dash nutmeg
Vegetable oil

Build a medium-hot fire, or set gas or electric grill to medium-high. Wipe fish inside and out with paper towels on a wooden board. Melt butter or margarine in a medium skillet; sauté onion until soft. Add spinach and cook 2 minutes. Add wine and bring to boiling; stir in bread cubes, salt, pepper and nutmeg. Stuff fish with spinach mixture; close opening with wooden skewers laced with cord; rub skin well with oil.

Place fish in a fish grilling rack, if you have one, for ease in turning. Grill, 10 to 20 minutes, brushing several times with oil. Turn grill rack or turn fish with 2 pancake turners. Grill 20 minutes longer, or until fish is firm. Place on heated platter. Garnish with lemon slices.

Marinated Fish

Makes 4 servings

1 lime
⅓ cup vegetable oil
1 tsp ground cumin
½ tsp ground coriander
¼ tsp granulated sugar
4 firm-fleshed fish steaks, such as halibut or swordfish

Blend finely grated peel and juice of 1 lime with vegetable oil, cumin, coriander and sugar. Place fish steaks in a dish just large enough to hold them snugly together. Pour juice mixture over top. Refrigerate for 2 hours, turning steaks often the first hour.

Drain steaks and place on preheated greased grill about 4" from hot coals. Barbecue about 10 minutes, turning at least once during this time and brushing frequently with marinade, until fish flakes easily with a fork.

Orange-Teriyaki Halibut Steaks

Makes 4 servings

4 halibut steaks, about 1" thick
¼ cup vegetable oil
¼ cup frozen orange juice concentrate
¼ cup soy sauce
¼ tsp ground ginger

Mix all ingredients and pour over fish steaks so all are covered. Marinate in fridge for 3 hours or on counter for 1 hour. Turn halfway through marinating.

To barbecue, place drained fish on a greased grill about 4" above hot coals. Close lid of barbecue. Barbecue for 10 to 15 minutes, turning often.

Barbecued Shark

Serves 3 - 4

Shark steaks, approximately ½ to ⅔ lb per person
3 Tbsp lime juice
5 Tbsp water
1 Tbsp sake or white wine
1 Tbsp olive oil
¼ - ½ tsp each garlic powder, chili powder
and cilantro flakes

Put steaks in non-metallic pan or bowl
with lime juice, water, sake and olive oil. Then
lightly sprinkle with garlic powder, chili
powder, and cilantro flakes. Let stand at room
temperature for about 15 minutes and then
turn. Sprinkle this side with the garlic powder,
chili powder and cilantro flakes as well. Let
stand 15 minutes then barbecue.

Magician's Memos

Recipe changes, additions, & doodles!

Accompaniments

Chilled Raspberry Soup

Makes 6 - ½ cup servings

1 ½ cups fresh raspberries or 425 g container frozen
unsweetened raspberries
1 cup (250 ml container) sour cream
¾ cup milk
Generous pinch of ground cardamom

Place fresh raspberries or entire contents of container of frozen
raspberries and sour cream in a food processor. Whirl, using and on-
and-off motion, until puréed.

Strain through a sieve to remove all seeds, if you wish. Stir in milk
until mixture is as thin as you like. Add cardamom. This soup will keep
in the refrigerator for several days. Serve garnished with fresh mint.

Potato Salad

Serves 6 - 8

2 ½ cups diced cold potatoes
1 tsp sugar
1 tsp vinegar
½ cup onion, chopped
1 ½ tsp salt
1 ½ tsp celery seed
¾ cup mayonnaise
2 hard-cooked eggs, sliced

Sprinkle sugar and vinegar over potatoes. Add rest of ingredients,
blending in eggs carefully. Serve in lettuce lined bowl. Garnish with
radishes, parsley, watercress, cucumber slices and egg slices.

For a change of pace and extra crunchiness you can add ½ cup
sliced celery, ¼ cup sliced sweet pickles. Chopped parsley in lieu of the
celery gives the salad color and a distinctive flavor. Make sure to keep
this cold until serving time.

Fresh Greek Salad

Makes 4 to 6 servings

1 small head romaine lettuce
½ head red-tipped lettuce
3 tomatoes
1 small un-peeled cucumber
1 small red onion
½ cup brine-cured black olives
½ cup feta cheese
½ cup olive oil
3 Tbsp freshly squeezed lemon juice
2 large garlic cloves, crushed
1 tsp whole oregano
Generous pinches of salt and freshly ground black pepper
2 anchovies (optional)

Wash lettuce and pat dry. Tear into bite-size pieces and place in a large salad bowl. Cut tomatoes into wedges. Thinly slice cucumber and onion, separating onion into rings. Scatter over top of greens along with olives. Rinse feta cheese well with cold water to remove excess salt. Crumble and sprinkle over salad.

In a small bowl, combine olive oil with lemon juice, garlic and seasonings. Finely chop anchovies and add to oil mixture. Whisk together until evenly blended. Drizzle over top of salad ingredients and toss together until all are evenly coated.

Spinach Salad

Serves 6 - 8

4 bunches of spinach
2 eggs, hard boiled
White vinegar or white wine vinegar to taste
3 - 4 strips of cooked bacon or bacon bits
Olive oil to taste
Cayenne pepper

Tenderly strip spinach leaves from root bases and clean. Spinach bruises easily, so be gentle. Rip into strips about ¾" wide and 3" long.

Chop egg and add to spinach with small pieces or bits of bacon. Refrigerate until ready to serve.

When ready to serve, drizzle a small amount of oil to very lightly coat spinach. Add a teaspoon or two of vinegar and a very light dusting of cayenne pepper to taste. Remember to keep out of sun or heat after preparation.

Traditional Caesar Salad

Use the Caesar dressing sparingly.

¼ cup oil
1 clove garlic, crushed
3 - 5 anchovies
2 - 3 Tbsp lemon juice
1 egg, raw or cooked gently for 60 - 90 seconds
¼ cup Parmesan cheese
1 head romaine lettuce, washed and dried
croutons
Parmesan cheese

Put the oil, garlic, anchovies, lemon juice, egg, and ¼ cup Parmesan cheese in a blender and blend at high speed until combined and fairly thick. Cut the romaine lettuce and place in a large salad bowl. Just before serving, add croutons and Parmesan cheese to taste, and just enough dressing to lightly coat the lettuce.

Coleslaw

½ - 1 whole green cabbage
¼ cup onion, diced, approximately
Mayonnaise or "Miracle Whip"
Paprika

Cut the green cabbage cut into strips approximately 1" long and approximately ⅛" wide. Place cut up cabbage in a bowl and add diced onion. Add enough mayonnaise or "Miracle Whip" to lightly coat all the cabbage. Sprinkle with Paprika, mix all together well and refrigerate until time to eat.

Traditional Greek Salad

Serves 4

1 small cucumber
½ small red onion
½ small green pepper
1 medium tomato
½ cup black Calamata Greek olives
½ cup feta cheese
½ cup olive oil
3 Tbsp lemon juice
1 tsp oregano flakes
2 cloves garlic, crushed

Combine olive oil, lemon juice, oregano and garlic in small bowl.

Cut vegetables into bite-size pieces and combine in a large bowl. Cut feta cheese in bite-size pieces and add with olives to vegetables. Cover with dressing and serve. This can be combined a couple of hours before serving and refrigerated.

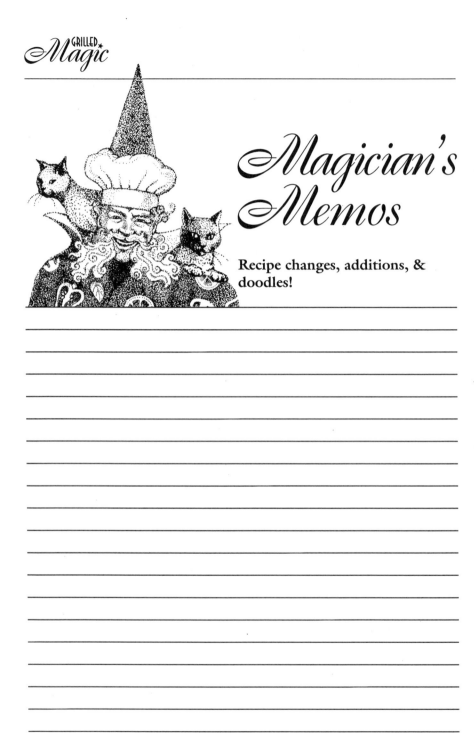

Magician's Memos

Recipe changes, additions, & doodles!

Vegetables

Vegetable Kebabs

Makes 4 servings

Garlic rice

1 Tbsp butter
2 garlic cloves, minced
1 cup long-grain rice
2 ½ cup chicken stock or bouillon

Spiced Rice

1 Tbsp butter
1 Tbsp oregano
½ Tbsp each thyme and sage
½ tsp salt
1 cup long grain rice
2 cups chicken stock or bouillon
½ cup white wine

Kebabs

1 small zucchini
1 small red onion
1 small green pepper
Cherry tomatoes
¼ lb small button mushrooms

Tahini Dip

¼ cup tahini (sesame paste)
¼ cup vegetable oil
1 tsp ground cumin

Yogurt Dip

¼ cup yogurt
⅛ cup blended cottage cheese
1 tsp paprika

Prepare rice by melting butter in a large saucepan. Add garlic or spices and sauté over low heat for a couple of minutes. Add rice and stir until evenly coated with butter. Add stock and bring to a boil. Cover, reduce heat and simmer until rice is tender, about 25 minutes.

Prepare kebabs by slicing up-peeled zucchini into ½" rounds. Cut onion and green pepper into thin wedges. Alternate vegetables colorfully on wood or metal skewers (watch when you remove, they're hot.)

Prepare Tahini Dip by whisking tahini with oil and cumin. Set aside at room temperature. Prepare Yogurt Dip by combining all ingredients in a blender at high.

Place kebabs on greased grill, about 4" above hot coals. Barbecue until vegetables are hot, turning kebabs often, about 4 to 6 minutes.

Place grilled vegetables on hot rice and drizzle with Tahini Dip or Yogurt Dip.

Garlic Potatoes

Makes 6 servings

6 potatoes
6 tsp butter, separated
3 small garlic cloves, thinly sliced
black pepper, freshly ground

Scrub 6 potatoes but do not peel. Place each potato, cut into ¼" slices, on an individual piece of thick foil. Dot each potato with 1 teaspoon butter. Thinly slice 3 small garlic cloves. Scatter several slices over each cut potato. Sprinkle generously with freshly ground black pepper. Gather up ends of foil and wrap up potatoes tightly.

Tuck foil packages into heated barbecue coals or place on a grill about 3" above hot coals. Barbecue for 25 minutes, turning occasionally, or until potatoes feel tender when pierced with a fork.

Fast 'N' Simple Vegetable Kebabs

Garden-fresh vegetables cook to perfection over the coals. Optionally, use parboiled new potatoes or large fresh mushrooms.

Makes 6 servings

1 lb small white onions
2 medium zucchini, cut into chunks
1 pint cherry tomatoes, halved
1 large green pepper, seeded and cut into squares
1 large red pepper, seeded and cut into squares
¼ cup butter or margarine
2 tsp chopped chives
1 tsp dill
1 tsp salt
¼ tsp lemon pepper

Parboil onions and zucchini in boiling salted water in a small saucepan 5 minutes; drain and cool; peel and, if large, halve onions.

Thread 6 long skewers with onion and cherry tomatoes, alternately with green pepper squares and chunks of zucchini and red pepper.

Melt the butter or margarine in a small saucepan; stir in chives, dill, salt and lemon pepper.

Grill kebabs, 4" from heat, turning and brushing several times with butter mixture, 15 minutes, or until vegetables are crisp-tender.

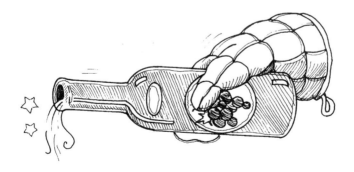

Marinated Broccoli & Red Peppers

Makes 6 servings

1 bunch broccoli
3 red peppers
2 Tbsp vegetable oil
2 Tbsp soy sauce
1 Tbsp red wine vinegar
1 Tbsp red wine

Remove heavy stalks from the broccoli, and then cut the remaining broccoli into fleurettes. Halve, seed and slice peppers and combine with broccoli fleurettes.

Place vegetable oil, soy sauce, vinegar and wine in a jar, cover with lid and shake vigorously to blend. Pour over broccoli and red peppers, tossing gently to blend. Cover with plastic wrap and let stand 1 hour, to blend flavors.

Fried Onion Rings

Makes 6 servings

1 ½ cups all purpose flour
1 can (12 oz) beer
1 tsp sage
3 very large yellow or white onions
2 to 3 cups vegetable shortening
salt and pepper

Combine flour, beer and sage in a large glass or ceramic bowl with a wire whip until well blended. Cover with plastic wrap and allow batter to rest at room temperature about 3 hflavors. (This makes the batter extra light.)

Cut onions into ¼" thick slices; separate slices into rings and remove the skin from the rings. Melt enough shortening in a 10" heavy skillet over low heat to a depth of 2"; heat to 375°F. Dip a few onion rings into batter, and let excess drip off them; carefully place them in the hot fat. Fry rings, turning once or twice, 3 minutes, or until golden brown, then transfer to a paper towel lined cookie sheet and keep warm in preheated oven. Continue until all the onion rings are fried.

These may be frozen. Fry rings and drain on paper towels at room temperature. Arrange on cookie sheet and freeze. When frozen, pack in plastic bags and return to freezer. To reheat arrange onion rings on cookie sheet. Heat in a hot oven (400° F) 4 to 6 minutes, or until hot.

Hot Curried Onions

Makes 2 cups

6 onions
⅓ cup butter
½ tsp ground thyme
1 tsp curry powder
½ cup regular beer
½ tsp Worcestershire sauce

Thinly slice onions and separate into rings. Melt butter in a large wide frying pan. Stir in onions and thyme. Sprinkle with curry. Sauté over medium-low heat until onions are soft, about 5 minutes. Stir occasionally. Then stir in beer and Worcestershire and boil gently over medium heat, uncovered, until onions are golden and pan juices are almost evaporated, about 8 minutes. Stir occasionally near end of cooking to prevent onions from sticking. Serve warm over patties.

Herbed Tomatoes

Makes 6 servings

6 large firm tomatoes
salt and pepper
2 Tbsp olive or vegetable oil
¼ cup chopped parsley
⅓ cup grated old cheddar cheese (or Parmesan)

Cut tomatoes into wedges. Season with salt and pepper. Drain on paper towelling 10 minutes. Arrange tomatoes in a heavy metal baking pan; drizzle with oil and sprinkle with chopped parsley; cover with heavy-duty aluminum foil. Place covered pan to back of grill and cook 10 minutes, or until tomatoes are tender; sprinkle with cheese. Serve hot or at room temperature.

Vegetable Bouquet

Makes 12 servings

2 bunches green onions
2 large yellow squash
black olives

Trim green onions and cut lengthwise into thin shreds; place in bowl of ice water. Trim squash and cut into long sticks; place in plastic bag.

At serving time, arrange green onions, squash sticks and black olives on a serving tray.

Onion-Potato Barbecue

6 potatoes

½ cup butter or margarine, softened
3 medium onions, thinly sliced
Grated Parmesan or cheddar cheese

Wash potatoes and cut in half lengthwise. Score the flat side of each half potato 2 or 3 times the length of the potato and 4 or 5 times across. Spread with softened butter or margarine and season with salt and pepper. Cover half with thinly sliced onions; sprinkle with grated cheese. Top with other potato half and place on sheet of heavy duty aluminum foil.

Brush potato skins lightly with oil and wrap tightly. Lay potatoes on grill and barbecue 45 to 60 minutes, turning several times.

Potatoes are done if they feel soft when pressed with an insulated glove.

Roast Corn

Corn
Butter
Salt and Pepper

Select tender sweet corn in the husks. Strip husks down to end of cob. Do not tear off. Remove silk. If desired, let stand in salted ice water 20 minutes to 1 hour, then drain well.

Brush corn with softened butter and sprinkle with salt and pepper. Bring husks up around corn. Secure with thin florist's wire, if necessary. Be sure entire ear is covered. Lay corn on grill over hot coals and barbecue 10 to 12 minutes. Turn a quarter turn 4 times during barbecuing. Husk will be brown and dry when corn is done. Remove husk and serve.

Magician's Memos

Recipe changes, additions, & doodles!

Sauces & Marinades

Kent's Sauce

Makes approximately 1 ½ cups

¼ cup melted butter or margarine
½ cup Worcestershire sauce
½ cup lemon juice
¼ cup or less white vinegar, to taste
2 Tbsp powdered mustard
1 Tbsp Tabasco sauce
½ tsp garlic powder
½ tsp onion salt
Black pepper

Add all ingredients in a pot and let simmer about 5 minutes, then cool and store a minimum of 2 hours. Vinegar is "to taste" and can be substituted with white wine. More Tabasco can be used for a "hotter" sauce. This sauce can be used as a marinade or a baste for all kinds of barbecued meats.

Chuckwagon Ranch Sauce

Makes approximately 4 cups

3 cups (24 oz) tomato sauce
2/3 cup brown sugar
½ cup ketchup
1/3 cup vinegar
4 Tbsp dry prepared mustard
1 cup chopped onion
2 chopped garlic cloves
3 Tbsp chili powder

Combine all ingredients in a pan and let simmer for 5 minutes. More chili powder can be added to make the sauce "hotter". This can be used as a marinade or a baste for all kinds of barbecued meats.

Basil Mayonnaise

Makes 1 ½ cups
2 eggs, at room temperature
2 Tbsp freshly squeezed lemon juice
1 garlic clove, crushed
¼ tsp salt
Freshly ground black pepper
1 cup vegetable oil
⅓ cup fresh basil leaves or 2 Tbsp dried basil

Measure all ingredients into a blender or food processor except oil and fresh herbs. Blend, using an on-and-off motion, until well blended. Continuing to mix, add oil, drop by drop at first, then increase to a thin stream until all oil is added. Add basil.

When creamy, turn into a jar and seal. Mayonnaise can be refrigerated for several days if you wish. Flavor improves with a day's refrigeration.

Serve on fresh grilled salmon, burgers or sandwiches.

Lemon Barbecue Sauce

Use this lively lemon-based sauce to perk up chicken and other poultry.

Makes ¾ cup

½ cup lemon juice
¼ cup vegetable oil
1 large clove garlic
1 tsp salt
½ tsp celery seed
½ tsp dried thyme, crumbled

Combine lemon juice and oil in small bowl. Mash garlic in salt and add to lemon juice mixture with celery seed and thyme, blending well. Let stand at room temperature overnight. Brush or pour over chicken or other poultry.

Marinade for Fish Steaks

This tangy marinade will enhance the taste of any firm-fleshed fish.

Makes 1 cup

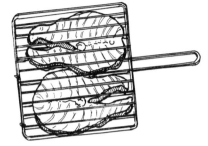

½ cup vegetable oil
⅓ cup soy sauce
¼ cup bottled lemon juice
2 tsp Dijon mustard
1 tsp grated lemon rind
1 clove garlic, minced

Combine oil, soy sauce, lemon juice, Dijon mustard, grated lemon rind and minced garlic in a small bowl, blending well. Pour over fish steaks in glass baking dish; marinate in refrigerator 3 hours before grilling.

Orange Sauce for Pork

A spicy accompaniment to fresh or smoked ham or spare ribs.

Makes about 1 ½ cups

3 oranges
3 small green chilies, seeded and minced
¼ cup water or white wine
2 tsp plum sauce or chutney
3 Tbsp vinegar
3 Tbsp sugar
¼ tsp salt
⅛ tsp dried oregano, crumbled

Squeeze juice from oranges into a small bowl; use a sharp-edged spoon to remove pulp and add to juice. Add minced chilies, water or wine, vinegar, sugar, salt and oregano, blending well. Let stand 1 hour. Serve with pork.

Mexican Barbecue Sauce

Use as a basting sauce for grilled meats with a South-of-the-Border touch.

Makes about 2 ½ cups

1 cup onion, chopped
½ cup olive oil
2 large ripe tomatoes, chopped
1 chili pepper, seeded and minced
2 tsp salt
1 clove garlic, crushed
¼ cup vinegar
¼ cup water
2 Tbsp chili powder

Sauté chopped onion in 2 Tbsp of the oil in small skillet over coals. Stir in tomatoes, chili, salt and garlic. Simmer over low heat until very thick, stirring often to prevent burning. Stir in remaining olive oil, the vinegar, water and chili powder, blending well. Cook over moderate heat 10 minutes, stirring constantly. Use as a basting sauce for grilled or roasted meats.

Beer Barbecue Sauce

Here's a tangy sauce that you can make over the coals while grilling meat.

Makes 3 ¼ cups

1 ½ cups tomato purée
1 can (12 oz) beer
¼ cup cider vinegar
3 Tbsp Worcestershire sauce
1 tsp salt
1 tsp hot paprika
½ tsp seasoned pepper

Combine tomato purée, beer, vinegar, Worcestershire sauce, salt, paprika and seasoned pepper in a small sauce-pan with a flameproof handle, blending well. Heat to a simmer over grill. Stir and continue simmering about 5 minutes. Brush over chicken or pork every 5 minutes after meat has cooked for 20 minutes.

Marinade for Lamb

Extra flavorful, this marinade doubles as a baste while grilling the lamb.

Makes 2 cups

1 cup dry red wine
½ cup olive oil
2 Tbsp minced parsley
2 Tbsp chopped chives
2 cloves garlic, crushed
½ tsp Worcestershire sauce
¼ tsp pepper
dash *each* dried marjoram, rosemary and thyme, crumbled

Combine wine, olive oil, parsley, chives, Worcestershire sauce, pepper, marjoram, rosemary and thyme in small bowl, blending well. Pour over butterflied leg of lamb in glass dish and let stand in refrigerator overnight. Use marinade to baste lamb several times during last 25 minutes of grilling on each side.

Bleu Cheese Butter

This tangy butter enhances the flavor of the burgers and steaks and can be used for other meats as well.

Makes ¾ cup

½ cup bleu or Roquefort cheese
¼ cup butter or margarine, softened
2 Tbsp sherry, white wine, brandy or cream

Remove cheese and butter or margarine from refrigerator. Crumble the cheese. Allow both to stand at room temperature about 1 hour.

Mash cheese with butter in a small bowl with a fork. Stir in sherry, wine, brandy, or cream and mix to a smooth paste. Turn into a bowl. Serve at room temperature on beef of all kinds or chicken breasts.

Tandoori Dipping Sauce

Makes about 2 cups

2 cup plain yogurt
1 to 3 Tbsp curry powder
1 green onion, finely chopped

Combine all ingredients a small bowl. Refrigerate overnight. Serve with smoked turkey.

Hot Mustard Sauce

Makes ⅔ cup

⅓ cup prepared hot mustard or Dijon mustard
¼ cup sour cream or mayonnaise
¼ to ½ tsp Tabasco sauce
Pinch of granulated sugar (optional)

Combine mustard, sour cream and ¼ tsp Tabasco in a small bowl. Stir together until blended. Taste and add more Tabasco and a pinch of sugar if you wish.

Gonzales Mexican Sauce

Makes ¾ cup

¼ cup strong coffee
¼ cup ketchup
¼ cup Worcestershire sauce
2 Tbsp cider vinegar
⅛ cup brown sugar
1 tsp chili powder
½ tsp dry mustard

Combine all ingredients in a small heavy-bottomed saucepan. Blend together over medium heat and bring to a boil. Then cover, reduce heat and simmer for 15 minutes to thoroughly blend flavors. Stir occasionally.

Serve as a sauce over burgers, steaks or chops. Or work into burgers before grilling.

Citrus Marinade

Makes about 1 cup

¼ cup fresh lemon juice
¼ cup fresh lime juice
¼ cup olive oil
½ cup onion, finely chopped
Freshly ground pepper
½ tsp dried dill weed
½ tsp dried tarragon
½ tsp sugar

Combine all ingredients in jar with tight fitting lid. Shake well and use as marinade and basting sauce for barbecued fish or seafood.

Orange Soy Marinade

Makes 2 ½ cups

2 cups orange juice
½ cup soy sauce
½ cup green onions, chopped
1 tsp salt
1 tsp sugar
½ tsp ground ginger

In medium bowl, combine all ingredients. Use as a marinade and basting sauce for fish, chicken, spareribs or ham.

Ginger Marinade

Makes 1 ½ cups

½ cup soy sauce
⅓ cup maple syrup
⅓ cup dry sherry
1 garlic clove, crushed
1 tsp grated fresh ginger root

In saucepan, combine all ingredients. Stirring constantly, bring the mixture to a boil over moderate heat. Reduce heat and simmer for 5 minutes. Remove from heat and cool. Use as a marinade and basting sauce for chicken or pork.

Basic Basting Sauce

Makes 4 cups

¼ cup olive or salad oil
¾ cup onions, chopped
1 clove garlic, chopped
1 cup honey
1 cup ketchup
1 cup wine vinegar
½ cup Worcestershire sauce
1 Tbsp dry mustard
1 ½ tsp salt
1 tsp oregano
1 tsp black pepper
½ tsp thyme

Heat oil in saucepan; sauté chopped onion and garlic until tender. Add all remaining ingredients and bring to a boil, stirring constantly. Cook another 5 minutes very slowly.

This all purpose sauce can be poured into sterilized jars, sealed and stored and is perfect for basting hamburgers, steaks, wieners, spareribs, chops and ham steaks.

Red Wine Marinade

Makes 3 cups

2 cups red wine
¼ cup vinegar or lemon juice
1 onion, sliced
¼ cup onion, chopped
½ cup carrot, chopped
Few peppercorns
2 bay leaves
parsley
1 tsp thyme

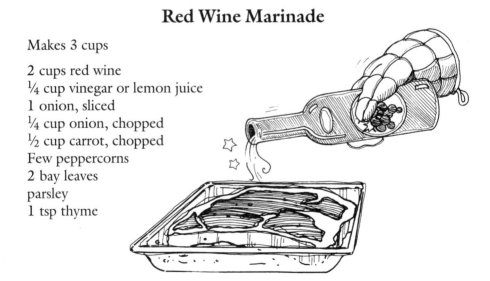

Combine all ingredients in saucepan, bring to a boil, cover and simmer for 10 minutes; strain and allow to cool. Place meat in marinade and leave from 6 to 24 hours, turning occasionally. The length of time will depend on the size of the meat; e.g. a 6-pound moose roast should be marinated 24 hours. To use for basting, add 1 cup of oil.

For rabbit, game, and less tender cuts of meat.

Herb Flavored Wine Sauce

Makes 1 ½ cups

1 small garlic clove, crushed
fresh tarragon
fresh thyme
fresh rosemary
1 cup dry white wine, rosé or sherry
1 tsp salt
½ tsp freshly ground pepper
dash Tabasco sauce
½ cup butter

Crush the garlic in a small saucepan. Add a few springs of fresh tarragon, thyme and rosemary, bruising them with garlic.

Pour in the white wine, rosé or sherry and add salt, pepper, and Tabasco. Add butter and heat but do not boil.

Steep ingredients for about 10 minutes, strain and use.

Basic Marinade #2

Makes 3 ½ cups

1 ½ cups oil
¾ cup soy sauce
¼ cup Worcestershire sauce
2 Tbsp dry mustard
2 ¼ tsp salt
⅓ cup fresh lemon juice
1 Tbsp pepper
½ cup wine vinegar
1 ½ tsp dried parsley flakes
2 garlic cloves, crushed, if desired

Combine all ingredients and mix well. Store in a tightly-covered jar in freezer indefinitely or in refrigerator for about a week.

Lemon Basting Sauce #2

Makes 1 ½ cups

¾ cup butter
2 tsp paprika
1 tsp sugar
1 tsp salt
½ tsp black pepper
¼ tsp dry mustard
½ cup lemon juice
½ cup hot water
Few grains cayenne pepper
Few drops Tabasco
2 Tbsp grated onion (if desired)

Melt butter, add paprika, sugar, salt, black pepper, mustard and cayenne pepper. Blend in water and lemon juice. Add Tabasco and grated onion, if desired.

Simple Barbecue Sauce

Makes 1 ½ cups

½ cup oil
¾ cup lemon juice or cider vinegar
¼ cup water
1 Tbsp salt
3 Tbsp brown sugar

Heat above ingredients together and keep hot for basting chicken. Mix thoroughly before each basting.

If you prefer a highly seasoned sauce, add a dash of Tabasco, dry mustard and Worcestershire sauce.

Quick Barbecue Sauce

Makes 2 cups

1 cup ketchup
1 cup tomato juice
½ tsp Tabasco sauce
2 Tbsp vinegar
3 Tbsp brown sugar
1 tsp dry mustard
2 tsp salt
2 tsp paprika
½ tsp pepper
½ cup mild onion, finely chopped
4 Tbsp butter or margarine

Combine all ingredients. Simmer for 5 minutes.

GRILLED

Chris' Barbecue Sauce

Makes 2 cups

¼ cup margarine
½ cup onion, chopped
1 tsp salt
½ tsp pepper
1 tsp paprika
2 Tbsp brown sugar
¼ tsp garlic salt
1 cup ketchup
½ cup water
¼ cup lemon juice or vinegar
1 Tbsp Worcestershire sauce
2 dashes Tabasco sauce

Melt the margarine, add chopped onion and cook until onions are transparent. Add remaining ingredients and simmer for 10 minutes.

Caribbean Barbecue Sauce

Makes ¾ cup

½ cup table molasses
¼ cup prepared mustard
3 Tbsp vinegar
2 Tbsp Worcestershire sauce
½ tsp Tabasco
1 tsp ground ginger
2 Tbsp soy sauce

Blend molasses and mustard. Add remaining ingredients; mix well.

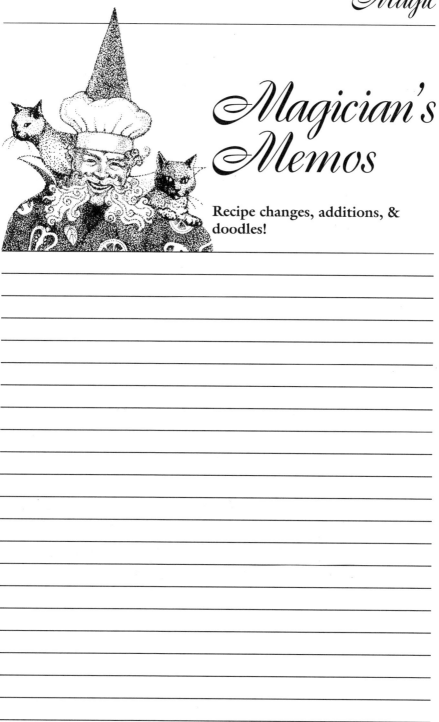

GRILLED
Magic

Magician's Memos

Recipe changes, additions, & doodles!

Appendix

	Smoked Light White Fish	Smoked Fatty Fish	Smoked Meats Beef Products
Chart 1 *Storage Life of General Types of Smoked Fish and Beef in Deep Freeze Conditions*			
At 15°F **Good** **Inedible**	1 month 3 months	3 weeks 2 months	1 month 2 months
At -5°F **Good** **Inedible**	3.5 months 10 months	2 months 5 months	3 months 8 months
At -29°F **Good** **Inedible**	4.5 months 7 months	9 months About 1 year	10 months Over 1 year

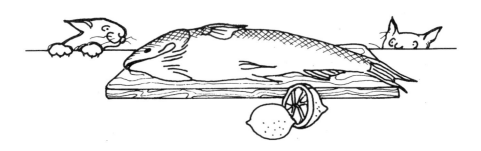

Chart 2 Outdoor Grill Timetable – Meats Approximate times		
		Minutes
Beef Steak 1" Thick	Rare Medium Well Done	8 to 12 12 to 15 up to 20
1 ½" Thick 2" Thick	Rare Medium Well Done Rare Medium Well Done	10 to 14 14 to 18 up to 25 18 to 30 25 to 35 up to 60
Lamb Chops 1" Thick 2" Thick		12 to 18 15 to 25
Chicken, Split		25 to 45
Ham Steaks ½" Thick 1" Thick		25 to 30 30 to 35
Hamburgers		10 to 12
Wieners (Hot Dogs)		6 to 8

Check doneness by a small knife cut near the bone. Time varies. Practice makes you an expert. Keep records for future reference.

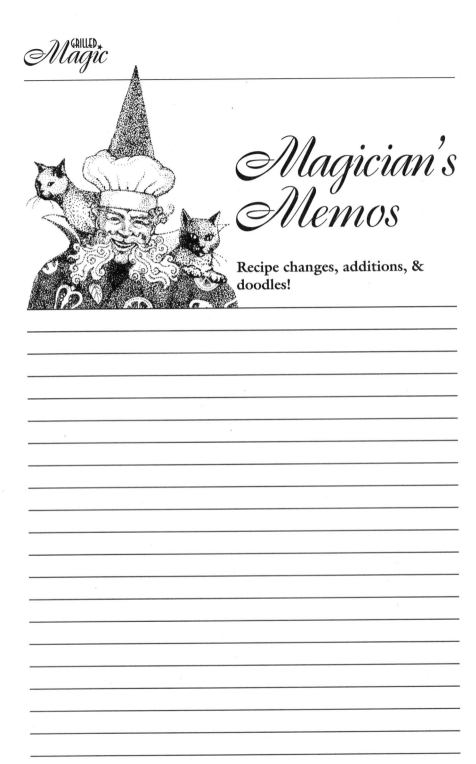

Magician's Memos

Recipe changes, additions, & doodles!

Chart 3			
Outdoor Grill Timetable – Vegetables			
Vegetable	**Preparation**	**Method**	**Seasoning**
Artichokes	Snip off top third and tops of leaves.	Wrap in foil and place on grill over even, but not hot, heat (not in centre of grill) for approximately 50 - 60 minutes or until artichoke can be pierced.	Drizzle butter, a touch of white wine, garlic salt and Parmesan cheese on before cooking.
Carrots	Trim tops and ends then scrub or peel with a vegetable peeler.	Wrap in foil and cook 10 - 15 minutes or until tender.	Butter with a little dill.
Corn	Remove the husk and silk. Wrap in husks to protect the kernels.	Don't put on the hottest part of the barbecue. Cook for 12 - 20 minutes. Fork will pierce part of husk when ready.	Butter, salt and pepper to taste.
Mushrooms	Wipe with a damp towel or a mushroom brush. Trim stem but leave whole.	Either wrap in foil and cook for 10 - 15 minutes or make kebabs and cook for 5 - 10 minutes.	Italian dressing, olive oil with lemon juice, butter or margarine, dill.
Onions	Peel skin and slice or chop for use with other vegetables either in foil pouch or in kebabs. Or leave skin on and cook directly on grill.	Whole, wrapped in foil cook 20 - 25 minutes. Sliced on greased foil about 5 minutes per side. Cubed in kebabs, about 10 - 15 minutes.	Butter or margarine, Italian dressing, olive oil with oregano, lemon butter, basil or nutmeg.

Vegetable	Preparation	Method	Seasoning
Red or Green Bell Peppers	Core ,remove seeds. Cut in half or in cubes for kebabs. Leave whole.	Wrapped in foil 15 - 20 minutes or until tender. In kebabs 10 - 15 minutes.	Italian dressing, olive oil with oregano, lemon butter, basil.
Potatoes	Scrub and pierce with fork. Leave whole or slice.	Whole, wrapped in foil 50 - 60 minutes or until tender when pierced. Or, sliced on greased foil about 15 minutes per slice.	Butter or margarine, chives, dill, sour cream, yogurt, grated Cheddar cheese, baste with oil and seasons or Italian dressing.
Summer Squash	Slice lengthwise or horizontally.	Wrapped in foil 20 - 25 minutes or until tender. Or, 10 - 15 minutes in kebabs.	Butter or margarine, chives, basil, Italian dressing.
Winter Squash	Cut in half, remove seeds, place cut side down on grill.	Cook 40 - 45 minutes or until tender.	Butter or margarine, nutmeg, brown sugar.
Tomatoes	Core and quarter large tomatoes or use cherry tomatoes for kebabs.	Cook kebabs 20 - 25 minutes or until soft.	Drizzle with vegetable oil or olive oil and basil, dill and oregano. Add grated Parmesan cheese 5 minutes before removing from grill.

Magician's Memos

Recipe changes, additions, & doodles!

Chart 4		
Metric and Imperial Conversion Tables		
Capacity	1 gallon	4.55 litres
	1 litre	0.22 gallon
	1 pint	0.57 litre
	1 litre	1.76 pints
	1 teaspoon	5 millilitres
	1 tablespoon	15 millilitres
	1 cup	250 millilitres
	¾ cup	175 millilitres
	½ cup	125 millilitres
	⅓ cup	75 millilitres
	¼ cup	50 millilitres
Weight	1 pound	0.45 kg
	1 kg	2.20 lb
	1 oz	28.35 g
	10 g	0.35 oz
Temperature	To convert Fahrenheit to Celsius, subtract 32, then multiply by 5 and divide by 9.	
	To convert Celsius to Fahrenheit, multiply by 9,	

Index

G

Gas Lines 17
Gazpacho Soup 51
Geography 7
Glazing 22
Grease 17
Grill 10, 18
  Basting 18
  Cleaner 13
  Fish 18
  Heating 18
  Height 10
  Hinged 13
  Type 10
  Variable Height 8
Grill Basket 17
Guacamole 50

H

Halibut
  Marinated Fish 95
  Orange-Teriyaki Halibut
    Steaks 95
Ham
  Ham with Basil Mustard 82
  Sweet & Sour Ham Steak 81
Heating Areas 8
Heating Racks 18
Hibachi 7, 9
Hickory 22
Horseradish and Caper Dip 53
Hot Dogs
  Barbecued Hot Dogs 90
Hot Salsa 48
Humidity 24

J

Japanese 9

K

Kebabs 9, 19
  Beef and Veggie 70
  Beef Kebabs 71
  Chicken Kebabs 76

Fast 'N' Simple Vegetable
  Kebabs 105
Okanagan Barbecue 70
Seafood Kebabs 93
Surf 'N' Turf 69
Vegetable Kebabs 103

L

Lamb
  Barbecued Lamb Leg 88
  Grilled Lamb Steaks 87
  Lamb Greek Style 87
  Marinade for Lamb 115
Lava Rocks 14, 17
Lemon Garlic Sauce 33
Lid 10
Liquid Starters 16
Location 7, 10

M

Maintenance 17
Marinades
  Basic Marinade #2 120
  Citrus Marinade 117
  Ginger Marinade 117
  Marinade for Fish Steaks 113
  Marinade for Lamb 115
  Marinade for The Ribs 43
  Orange Soy Marinade 117
  Red Wine Marinade 118
Mayonnaise
  Basil Mayonnaise 112
Meat Thermometer 13
Mesquite 22
Mushrooms 127
  Vegetable Kebabs 103
Mustard
  Hot Mustard Sauce 116

O

Onions 127
  Fast 'N' Simple Vegetable Ke-
    babs 105
  Fried Onion Rings 106
  Hot Curried Onions 107
  Onion-Potato Barbecue 108